The River Flows
As The
Mountains Watch

Deschutes
Memories

Copyright © 2000 by Retired and Senior Volunteer Program (RSVP)
Edited by Judy Osgood, Sunriver, Oregon
Published by RSVP, Bend, Oregon

Illustrated by Denise Mahoney and John O'Brien, Bend, Oregon
Cover by John O'Brien, Bend, Oregon
Book Design and Layout by Terry McShane, Chris Miao, and Linda West
Photo Credits: Submissions by story authors and Michael Houser
KBND Interviews by Deschutes County Historical Society

The contents of this book are a collection of memories of long-time Deschutes County residents. These oral histories were recorded by volunteers. The objective is to foster a sense of community and connection through first-hand accounts of local history. RSVP does not assume liability for the accuracy of this information.

ISBN: 0-9704990-0-0
Published and printed in the United States of America
First Printing, 2000

Acknowledgments

RSVP would like to thank the following volunteers for their invaluable assistance:

Executive: Beth Evans, Terry McShane, Helen Rastovich and Judy Osgood

Editorial: Judy Osgood

Interviewers & Writers: Charlene "Chuckie" Blahnik, Dave Blahnik, Lorna Cerenzia, Sandra Croney, Anne Elkin, Beth Evans, Michael Houser, Carol Illinik, Benjamin D. Malczewski, Art Marshall, George McGeary, Jim McGrath, Charleen McKee, Terry McShane, Raymond Miao, Ralph Morrison, Helen Rastovich, Shirley Ray, Carrie Sammons, Brooke Snavely, Martha Stranahan and Jo Ussery

Typing and Transcribing: Joan Craft, Beth Evans, Chuck Grossman and Clarissa Jurgensen

Art: Denise Mahoney and John O'Brien

Layout: Terry McShane

Historical Resource: Michael Houser, Helen Rastovich and Dan Rastovich

Sales/Marketing: Barbara Bosy, Dave King, Jim McGrath, Terry McShane, Ralph Morrison, Marie Phillis, Duane Radke and Helen Rastovich

Assistance: Jean Battelle, Beth Evans, Ray Miao, Marcella Radke and Gretchen Williver

Proof Readers: Chuck Grossman, Art Marshall, Jim McGrath, Pat Minney and Carrie Sammons

Brush Fire Suppression: Judy Osgood, Chuck Grossman and Ray Miao

Staff: Chris Miao, Pat Minney and Linda L. West

Special thanks to those who shared their stories. All of the information gathered served as a valuable resource.

The river races across the high desert, rising and falling as it follows the contours dictated by the volcanic activity millions of years before. It slows and widens to a beautiful pond that mirrors the images of the white-saddled mountains to the west. On the banks of this pond early inhabitants and settlers rested and later the towns grew. Out of the land and out of the people come stories–not all big stories, but all memories of what it was like to live in this beautiful country.

Ralph Morrison

These stories are first-hand memories distilled over time.
They have been recorded as they were told.

Proceeds from the sale of this book are used to sustain RSVP programs.

Retired and Senior Volunteer Program
St. Charles Medical Center
2500 NE Neff Road
Bend, OR 97701

(541) 388 - 7746

Preface

The men and women who homesteaded the Central Oregon country east of the Cascades between 1875 and 1920 were, for the most part, a hardy lot. Those who weren't rarely lasted long enough to tame the land and claim its promises. Addie Triplett, who gave birth to a daughter in a tent in the middle of Wall Street, summarized their success saying, "When we had to make do and depend on ourselves to get by, we did it." It is the stories of their making do and getting by that we have gathered here, for they are worth remembering and passing on.

Between 1920 and 1950 the population swelled with newcomers who were equally industrious, adventurous, and fun loving. Timber was the magnet that drew many of them to new jobs in the logging industry, while railroad advertising claiming there were riches to be made, lured many to homesteads on the high desert. Even then, some came primarily for the hunting and fishing. A few, like Sam and Becky Johnson, never intended to stay, but fell in love with the land and couldn't leave.

From the ordinary to the extraordinary, all their stories are special. Lee Maker's experiences driving the Mt. Hood Stage will bring a smile to your face, while the cougar that stalked Mac McKenzie may raise the short hairs on your head too. The stories of others like Maren Gribskov, Felix Marcoulier, Sister Catherine and Lowell Jensen tell the role they played in the creating of our well-loved establishments and institutions, the Pine Tavern, Mt. Bachelor and the St. Charles Medical Center.

It is with deep appreciation for their willingness to share their stories that we present *The River Flows as the Mountains Watch: Deschutes Memories*.

Judy Osgood
Editor

Table of Contents

A Coming-Back-To Place

As told by Don Blanding in 1953 to Kessler Cannon, KBND radio

Don Blanding, Bend's own widely known poet, writer, lecturer and humorist came to Bend in 1912 fresh out of high school in Lawton, Oklahoma. His cousin, Charlie Hudson, brought him out to work in the bank. "It didn't take me long to realize that I didn't like banking," he said, "but I certainly liked Bend. And it's been a coming-back-to place ever since." Bend nourished the spirit of this multi-talented man.

It was an exciting time in Bend when Blanding arrived, a pioneer stage that he described as the time in its history "where most of its past is in its future." He said that all the fathers, the men that he described as the city grandfathers were "young, eager bucks then just as I was . . . Ward Cole, Clyde McKay, Jimmy Overturf, and a little later Dutch Stover. We had great dreams and great visions of what this was going to be. We didn't have anything to work with, but we had a lot of work to do."

Blanding worked at the bank about a year and a half. "There weren't many strange faces in those days," he said, "cause after a week, you see, you belonged to the place. You didn't ask questions, but you kept your ears open for anything that might be dropped in the way of pasts." When he left Bend the first time it was to go to the Artists Institute in Chicago. As late as the '50's, some of his drawings were still in the old files of the Bulletin.

Periodically he came back to visit Ward and Ann Cole, and on one occasion he reminisced about recreation in Bend when he first lived here. "Oh, just staying alive was recreation," he said. Blanding told about a cow pasture near Drake Pond that served as a golf course of sorts. One day Don went down there to play with a friend, and reported that he lost three balls in the chipmunk or ground squirrel holes. In reply to the comment that it was surprising he even thought of golf in those days, he replied, "I didn't think much of it. The others did, but I didn't!"

Over the years the mountains were the magnets that drew him back. Once when he returned he was awfully tired and weary from five weeks of really roaring lecture tours and autograph parties, but as usual the magnificent Cascades and the area itself refreshed him. "Five days here," he stated, "will do the equivalent of a month's rest anywhere else. The smell of the sagebrush, and the place itself, and of course the Quack and Waddle Society...the ducks down in the pond helped me a great deal to recuperate." Then, as always, returning to his coming-back-to place was for Blanding, "a most joyous thing."

That sentiment has swelled the ranks of Central Oregon retirees in recent years as scores of men and women, who were privileged to live here at some point in their lives, have returned in retirement to their coming-back-to place.

Home on the Central Oregon Range

As told by Prince Staats in 1953 to Kessler Cannon, KBND radio

My dad, Billy Staats, came here to homestead in 1879. He had a pretty big spread on both sides of the Deschutes River that ran all the way from Bend down to where the Tumalo Bridge is now. In fact, where downtown Bend is located was our best cow pasture. It had an old brush fence that ran around it and it was chock full of bunch grass that really put the fat on the stock that we ran in there.

My mother, Emma Turpin, came here to visit her sister who was homesteading on the Hubbard Place. She met my dad and never did leave.

When my brother and I got old enough, we were sent to the old log schoolhouse that was located at the end of what is now Drake Park. Del Ireland, my cousin, was the teacher there for ten of us kids. We were all ages.

The first day of school my brother and I sat through all the lessons until recess. We got out of that one room and we thought, "Well, that's it for today!" and we made a beeline for home. When we came ambling in the yard of the home ranch, Mother caught sight of us and set us straight. We had to turn around and hightail it back to the schoolhouse.

It was a fair piece for us kids to walk and we weren't in too big a hurry to get back. Del didn't give us too warm a welcome when we straggled in or then, again, maybe he did, as he gave us both a pat on our backsides for our ignorance or to discourage it from happening again. He told us, next time, wait until you're told school is out before you light out for home.

For fun, there used to be good old hoe-downs (dances) where all ages, the young and the old, gathered together to socialize. Father was a fiddle player, a violinist, and he could play some tunes. Everybody traveled up river to Big Meadows, about where Sunriver is now. The dancing went on from sundown to sunup when we had breakfast the next day.

One day Mr. Drake came driving into the yard of our ranch head-quarters driving a fancy outfit. It was a regular house built on a wagon pulled by a team of horses. He had a man special to tend the team, do the cooking and just about anything else Drake wanted done.

Drake camped at our place and took a liking to Father's spread so he started fishing around to see if Father might sell. Dad just chuckled and threw out a price he thought was three times what it was worth. Well, Drake snapped it up and got all but the 10 acres our home was surrounded by. That was for $4,000!!! And Dad thought he'd really made a sale.

At that time emigrants were still coming through - either going or coming from California. They'd stop at our place for three days to a week to rest up from the bumpy wagon trek. Their wagons would come rolling in and the kids would come spilling out, and we'd have a big time while they were there with us.

My brother and I would ride horses to make money. Folks from back east would show up here and buy a few cayuses that had been rounded up from the horses running wild in the desert. Then they would need someone to ride them. Our standard price to ride those broncos was $3 a horse. We'd have to get a saddle on them and try and get it cinched down tight. A good many times I'd end up picking myself out of the dirt, but my brother's saddle never seemed to loosen up on any kind of a horse. He was quite the rider and didn't have to dust his britches off.

When we needed supplies, we'd harness up the team for a three-day drive to Prineville. We'd be hitched and headed out to Powell Butte in the rosy dawn before the day had a chance to heat up. The Vandevert place was on the side of Powell Butte. We'd show up there dusty and ready for a dipper of water. From Vandevert's to Prineville it was eight more miles, so if we were up plenty early we could get to Prineville, load up and get back to Vandevert's by dusk. Then, the next day, we'd drive back home to Bend.

Once a year in the fall, we'd go across McKenzie Pass to the Valley in a four-horse covered wagon. We'd go through Eugene to Albany and then on to Independence where we had relations. Coming back, the wagon would be stocked with fruit, flour, and sugar.

One year, Father was hired on as a cook for Pelton & Brown's cattle drive. Twenty cowboys rounded up 1500 head of cattle in the Klamath Reservation country. The cowboys drove them through Bend to The Dalles. It was an 18-day drive. Cattle could make about 10-15 miles a day, stirring up a great cloud of dust as they went.

My brother and I got to go along and we thought it was great sport. When we got hungry, we would leave the herd and hightail it to where the camp was set up for the night so Dad could feed us.

We would see the herd coming from a long ways off, the dust rising in a column. The first cattle walking lined out, then the rest coming in were bunched up. Those cows would start getting in about five in the evening and the last stragglers would plod in two hours later. It was a big procession coming along mooing and bellowing.

Two cowboys at a time would have to take shifts watching the night herd. Sometimes I'd wake nights and hear the stock lowing and hear the cowboys talking or singing low to settle the herd.

It was quite a time.

The Winter the Thermometer Froze
As told by W. E. Claypool in 1953 to Kessler Cannon, KBND Radio

Oh yes, I remember that big storm. The big storm, or the big snow as we sometimes called it, was in the winter of 1883-'84. Everybody seems to think it was the coldest winter we've ever had in this country as it froze up every thermometer that they had...it didn't register any deeper.

I went to school for the first time that year. My cousin, Mary Wheeler was the teacher. There were probably eight, maybe ten of us in a log cabin, 'bout where the high school in Sisters was in the '50's. Of course, there wasn't any town of Sisters then, just the post office at Camp Polk. Some of the students at the little school came from as far away as eight miles. School started in May and run three months, just in the summertime. That winter and most of the others, there was no way of breaking roads to go anywhere.

The day the storm hit, my father and his brother and an uncle had went out hunting, and they were out at what was called Three Creek Butte. They got snowed in out there, and my mother and I were by ourselves. My aunt lived on the adjoining place, and there was two children in their family, but we were snowed in so we couldn't even get from house to house. I did shovel a road to the hogs, and the chicken house. I remember that very well.

It was said there was six feet of snow that came down. And it laid 90 days. Just kept coming. Never stopped from the time it started 'til it got that depth, and just quit. It killed practically all the cattle and horses there was in the country. And then we had no rain or anything for oh, I'd say a month. It got cold. And the snow settled down and got a crust, and people would go out and these horses and cattle would be in what they called beats. They'd just have a place, corral, it'd be down, you know, and they'd shovel trails out, and they'd get them out of that and get them on top of the snow and they was quite a lot saved that way, taking them to feed. After you'd get them out, they could walk on the crust, but they'd been in there to a point that if you didn't shovel a road out for a ways to get them started, you couldn't get them out at all.

I remember one time my uncle and I went out and found some horses, and they were eating on a colt, and it was still alive. Yes it was. All the horses that was left the following spring had no manes or tails. They'd just ate the hair off just as close as you'd shave it, you know. I could take you over in the country and show you yet where they were beached. And you can see the bones of the horses there. Ate all the bark off the timber and trees and just as far up as they could, and of course the timber and stuff died then, and you can find a great many of those places over in that country yet.

That was quite a storm the winter of '83 - '84, one that none of us who lived through it will ever forget.

Life is a journey and not a destination.
If we make it a destination, we never get there.
The joy of the journey is what it's all about.
Rolf Benirschke, 1983 NFL Man of the Year.

There Wasn't Anything Easy About Homesteading

As told by Addie Triplett in 1953 to Kessler Cannon, KBND radio

We left North Carolina on a blustery day in March, 1902 and traveled to Shaniko. It was the jumping off place for this territory and there we boarded a big four-horse stagecoach for a rough, dusty drive to Prineville.

Arriving on a Saturday night, my husband, Carl, and his father set off through the bustling town of tents and shanties to find our friend Mr. Whitted who had written us about the government land homesteads. Carl wanted to look over the claims out by Whitted's place and find one for us.

Grandpa and I stayed in town with the baby while my husband caught a stage out into the desert area he wanted to look over. It was rough country back then and the stage broke down trying to make it up a steep grade out in the brush, so Carl took off cross-country on foot. After a night out there listening to the coyotes howl, he finally made it into Bend.

He filed on the claim he had found six miles south of Bend and the papers were processed in the United States Land Office at The Dalles. We didn't have the money then to buy our grubstake so Carl headed over to Ochoco to run a little gasoline engine that was used at the sheep shearing plant. It took him six weeks to get the cash we needed to buy a little square cook stove, two iron bedsteads and some rawhide bottomed chairs. He didn't buy a table because he figured he could make one out of the scraps of lumber left over from building our new cabin.

We set out at the break of dawn and even though it was June it was still plenty chilly. Our trunks and belongings were lashed on the wagon pulled by a team of horses that we had hired. In Bend we stopped to order lumber for our cabin. At that point Bend was just a rye field with the road running kitty-corner to it. The Pilot Butte Inn was an old boarded up building, and the only other structures in town were a little store and the Staats boarding house where the cattlemen stopped.

As we headed west across the Deschutes River it was rough going picking our way through the sheep trails and tracks. Night overtook us before we could find the turn off to Mr. Whitted's cabin where we had planned to spend the night. Being all tuckered out and confused, we stopped and bedded down under the stars figuring it would all look better in the morning.

The fellow who came with the hired wagon and horses didn't go to bed at all that night. He was worried that the hot, thirsty horses would bolt for the river because they could smell the water and he was also concerned about a grizzly bear prowling about whose scent would rile the horses. When daylight came he unloaded our gear, ate breakfast, and then left taking the team back to Prineville.

The rest of the way, we had to carry our gear. Though our claim was just across the Deschutes from Whitted's, we had to bushwhack two and a half miles down to the pole bridge to get across the river, and then backtrack to our claim. Grandpa and Carl told me it was best for me and little Charlie to wait there 'til they came back, but I said there was no way they were going to leave the baby and me alone there. So Grandpa took little 5-month-old Charlie; I carried the baby's things and we set off. There wasn't even a trail to follow through the brush and boulders. Finally, scraped and sweaty, we got to our claim. Then we had to make the trip a second time to get our bedding and blankets before dark.

Grandpa built a big bonfire and we fixed something to eat. After that he nailed boards to trees and laid more boards across them to give us some shelter until the cabin was hewn in. Once it was up, it took cutting down a few trees to find one that the grain was straight enough for us to cut shakes for the cabin. I never chopped any of the trees down, but I did use the crosscut saw to cut up firewood. I'd put little Charlie down on a blanket while I'd be working sawing, but it seemed like he'd always be crawling off so that put an end to my firewood business.

Grandpa worried the wood stove wouldn't be enough heat for the winter, so he set about building a fireplace and chimney. We lugged every rock down there for him. It was quite a job, but when it was finished the chimney stood for years. That winter there was four to five feet of snow. We never once got to town or even over the three miles to our closest neighbors, the Brocks.

My husband was working for the Irrigation Company building ditches. He only got home on Saturday nights. Grandpa and I held down the homestead for twenty months before we moved to Bend in January of 1904 and put up a tent where Brooks-Scanlon Mill is now. Bend was a bustling place then with people filing homestead and timber claims.

Later we got a lot over on Wall Street and moved the tent over there. Carl just wanted to get us closer to where he worked so he wouldn't have to travel so far. Our daughter was born in that tent in the middle of Wall Street just a little northeast of the Pilot Butte Inn.

Life was easier for us after we finished putting up a two-story building that had an apartment for us on the second floor. Neither homesteading or living in a tent in town was easy, so we appreciated the comforts that came with that move. However, I'll always remember those times and feel good about the fact that when we had to make do and depend on ourselves to get by, we did it.

Across the Plains and Over the Mountains

As told by Ruth Caldwell Coyner in 1953 to Kessler Cannon, KBND radio

My great grandparents came across the plains in 1848 during the gold rush years and settled in the Willamette Valley. They told an interesting story from their westward journey. At that time my grandfather was only six months old, and some Indians they encountered offered to trade a pony for him. Of course, you can imagine, my great grandmother had very few nights of rest after that time until they arrived in the Willamette Valley. My other great grandparents also came across the plains and my grandmother on that side of the family was native Oregonian.

My father and mother came to Bend from Albany in 1905 when I was nine. They chose Bend because it was being played up in the newspaper, and my father was a hunter and he had been over this way hunting and liked the area. We moved across the mountain by horse and wagon. It is interesting because it took us about 10 days to get here from Albany. We came with a four-horse team and wagon, heavily loaded, and there were two milk cows tied on behind. For that reason it was a very slow trip across the old South Santiam.

Every night we camped out and it was my duty to help peg the tent down with the little wooden sticks that my father would chop. We had to get out and walk up Seven-Mile Hill, and also up Sand Mountain. One of the brightest spots of that trip to me was the spring half way up Seven-Mile Hill, 'cause we could get a good, fresh drink of water.

Through the years, as we've gone back and forth over those highways, I could point out to my sons and say, "There's where we camped on such-and-such a night," and "There's where the wagon tipped over one time, and it went off in the mud hole!"

When I was growing up our picnics and our trips were the bright spots of our school activities. I remember my geology class in high school went on a field day up to Lava Butte and the Lava River Caves. Our transportation was a wagon with our lunch boxes and all the kids piled in it. We went through the caves in the morning, clear to the back and put our name in the bottle at the back of the cave. There was no path in those days; we just climbed over the rough rocks. It took about a pair of shoes for that trip. At noon we had our picnic dinner, and I remember that my chum, Faye DeArmond, got so cross at Harry Johnson that she threw a blackberry pie and hit him smack in the face with it! And then in the afternoon we climbed Lava Butte.

Although it wasn't a custom, our senior class took a senior trip. There were seven of us - five boys and two girls. Arthur, the youngest Vandevert boy, invited our class to go up to the old Vandevert homestead south of Sunriver at Christmas time for a house party. Mrs. Emerson Stockwell was our chaperone, and poor lady, I don't believe she's ever gotten over it! We had to go in a large wagon and I believe we had runners on that year because there was a lot of snow on the ground. It was very cold and we took bricks to keep us warm. Our cook was Billy Vandevert who made really good sourdough biscuits. What a trip that was!

After graduation I went to Oregon State where I was majoring in home economics. When the first World War started I came home from school for the summer and got such a good job with the mill that I didn't go back. I was the first female ever employed by Shevlin-Hixon.

I met Craig Coyner at an Epworth League social, and we were married the first time we met. Of course it was a mock wedding. They went out in the garden and pulled up pea vines for my bouquet. I had gone with George Vandevert, but I went to the next social with Craig, and as you can tell from my name, the day came when I really did marry him.

The water for drinking tasted so good.
Relatives from back east tried to take some home.

From Iris (Stewart) Wood

Apple Dumplings

2 cups flour   3 teaspoons baking powder
5 tablespoons oil   1/3 cup sugar
7/8 cup milk   1/2 teaspoon salt

Roll out dough, slice Gravenstein apples, add to dough with sugar, cinnamon, nutmeg, dots of butter.

Roll, cut in one inch thick sections. Place in pan (9x13), sprinkle with sugar, butter, cinnamon.

Pour boiling water over to 3/4 full, add vanilla.

Bake at 350 degrees about one hour.

Submitted by Cherri McKenzie from her Grammy Ida Newton who was born February 13, 1899 in Oregon. She died November 23, 1995 and is buried in the Hubbard Pioneer Cemetery.

Cherri remembers the wonderful smells of her Grammy's dumplings baking in the oven.

Vandevert Homestead in the Wilderness

As told by T.W. and Billie Vandevert in 1953 to Kessler Cannon, KBND radio

In 1892 my father, William Vandevert, took us in a horse drawn wagon from Fort Worth, Texas to Bend, Oregon. It was a long trip on small dirt roads and I sometimes rode our pony to keep the cow from lagging behind. Our route took us along the Columbia River to The Dalles and then headed inland to Prineville and Powell Butte. We had to spend the winter there and then moved on to the Bend area in May. Our first stop in Bend was to stay overnight at the Jim Montgomery homestead and cabin. His place was down near the present power dam.

The Bend area, which was then called Farewell Bend, was just homesteads and log cabins. There were only two roads in the area, one going east and west and one following the Deschutes River. Two bridges spanned the Deschutes, one at the Staats homestead where all the emigrants crossed and another at the Sizemore homestead.

My grandfather and two brothers were already settled in Bend, and when one brother heard that my father was coming he bought the Scoggin Homestead for him. Father then added to this by homesteading the adjoining property, all of which is known as the Vandevert Ranch. This land in the wilderness cost about $600 and included all the carpentry tools and a blacksmith shop.

15

Homesteaders often crossed the mountains to Eugene to sell products and get supplies. My father and brothers would sometimes take six horses and two wagons loaded with wool and come back with groceries. It took 21 days to make the trip, but there were many camp sheds for stopping to feed the horses and rest. Everyone enjoyed the trips with the camping and beautiful scenery. It was kind of a vacation and all the neighbors had to make the trip at least once a year.

Our school was very small and located near Colonel Besson's home. We would ride the pony three miles and at the start there were only three of us in the whole school. Our teacher was named Del Ireland and he was from over around Corvallis.

Fourth of July was always a big celebration around this area. Where Spring River feeds into the Deschutes River there is a big meadow and we had a party there. We had all kinds of food, people giving speeches, and foot racing. People came from all over to get acquainted and in the evening we would go over to the schoolhouse for dancing. We made ice cream and got the ice from the Dillman Cave near Sunriver. It seemed like everybody came from everywhere, for the dancing and entertainment.

The first house in Bend was the Drake house. The Drakes borrowed the broad saw from my father to hew the logs for it. Mr. Drake also built a bunkhouse and store by the park and river. Christmas of 1902 he held a community dance there. That night at his Christmas party he gave the community the first turkey I ever saw in Oregon.

Fishing was really good on the Deschutes River. You could see the fish everywhere and my father could catch about forty fish in a couple of hours using little trout flies. It was plenty of fish for two families.

In the early days Bend was mostly crooked wagon roads, and large timber. I've seen the timber disappear, the highways and railroad come, and the whole country change from what you might say was a beautiful wilderness to the present town.

Bend's Fun-Loving, Fashionable Schoolmarm

As told by Ann Markel Forbes in 1953 to Kessler Cannon, KBND radio

Pink cheeked, full of adventure and dreams of the wild and romantic West, my sister, Gertrude Markel, and I landed in Bend in August, 1909. We had traveled many miles after leaving Shaniko by stagecoach, and we arrived in Bend in the evening, stopping at the old Bend Hotel which is the Cashman Building located on the corner of Bond and Oregon Streets. Our first glimpse of the mighty men of the West was Hugh O'Kane who weighed 300 plus pounds. He was peacefully dozing in the late sunshine with his faithful dog at his feet. When Mr. O'Kane woke to give us a room, the little pooch was completely in the shadow of his master's enormous belly. We were broke, as we had never traveled before, and did not know how expensive it was. So we went to bed that night without any supper, except for some fruit which we had with us on the stagecoach. Luckily, we contacted Mr. Fred Ray, one of the school directors who had agreed to board and room us, so we could stave off our bill until payday. My sister, Trude, a stenographer, found employment a couple of days later in a local real estate office, and myself as a high school teacher- I made $75 a month.

The grade and high schools were housed in a frame building, which later burned, but was located then near the site of the present courthouse. Miss Ruth Reid was the principal of the high school, which was comprised of twenty pupils, and I was the other half of the faculty. No specializing for us! My subjects were English, German, Latin, and history. Miss Reid taught mathematics and science.

As I recall, there was a total of five teachers in those 12 grades, and we were kept very busy with teaching, school activities, and our social activities. After all, in the town of about 500 there were only a few women, and we schoolmarms were very necessary to the social life of the village. Perhaps we were considered a bit wild, for we loved to dance. According to one of the Baptist directors that was a grave sin, but our good friend, Fred Ray, overruled, and we were allowed to continue that activity. Basketball - albeit women's basketball - was another innovation in those days. Our team was composed of a few high school girls, and the rest were teachers and town girls. We were all "shockingly" garbed in full bloomer suits and black stockings. What would happen if we had appeared then in shorts! The town really supported our girls' team. I recall when we returned to Bend from a successful trip to Prineville, where we played the Prineville girls, we were met at the depot by a brass band, and also by the bank officials, who presented each one of us with a box of chocolates. What a thrill! That was surely a triumph!

Lara's Hall, which was above the old Penney Building on Wall Street, was the scene of all our festivities...dances, basketball, and box socials. These affairs were very well attended, especially by the young men who were working on the railroad survey. They caused many a feminine heart to flutter, and spurred us on to good basketball playing and expert two-stepping and waltzing. I recall when one of those stalwarts named George Palmer Putnam, who was a bit smitten on me, walked me to Lara's Hall with the aid of a lantern. This was quite necessary in those days to guide us over the rocks - there was no walks then. He forgot to put out the light, so in we march, with a lighted lantern, in illuminated view! This, George was teasingly reminded of on more than one occasion.

In romances though, things was not always so rosy. On one occasion, the boys had become a bit careless about waiting to the last minute to issue invitations to members of the Priscilla Club, which just happened to be all the young ladies of the town - about a dozen. So we decided in true pioneer fashion, to teach them that the pursuit of the female was not as easy as hunting deer. With much secrecy and diplomacy, we agreed to go home after Alice Allen's party just as we had arrived, with or without escorts. I confess that we really kept out of the boys' range - only two girls were asked - the rest of us thought it would be great fun to see their downcast and remorseful expressions.

Courage you say? Yes! What group of modern damsels would dare take such risks on losing their chance in the matrimonial game? Well, with much giggling and anticipation, we went to Alice Allen's party, let her in on the secret, and deposited our coats in her bedroom- the men had theirs in another room. After the games and eats, we filed into the bedroom, quickly donned our coats, and silently sped to our homes. Some of the boys loudly voiced their choice of partners; for instance, one insisted that he was taking the littlest Markel home. That was Gertrude. They waited and waited, shifted from one foot to another, and even searched under the beds. After a considerable length of time waiting, Alice asked them what they were hanging around for, and informed them that the girls had already gone home; that they had left just as they had come. Oh, such reactions! Some were furious; in fact, the one who wanted to take the littlest Markel home decided right then and there that he was through...never escorted her again! Some were more lighthearted and saw the funny side, as evidenced by the note I received for the next dance at Lara's Hall, which requested in a very formal way the pleasure of my company and so forth. After his signature, he designated himself as a "Member of the Waiter's Club," with a P.S.: "Lara's Hall has no back door!"

Picnics were also quite the fashion. We traveled in hacks; two seated horse bib and rigs, or rode horseback. And you should have seen our picnic outfits; ankle length skirts, shirtwaists with high neck and black ribbon bows, and large hats, secured by veils. A picture of the group on Pilot Butte, which we climbed quite often for fun and excitement, shows that garb. That's just another proof of the physical endurance and strength of the pioneer school-marms - and in such dress!

Some of the clothes were not always so modest though. As the fashion demanded shorter shirts, ours rose. One day when I was walking down Main Street clad in a new white outfit, which I considered quite natty, I was surprised to see our good Miss Mary Coleman stop dead in her tracks. She remained motionless with eyes glued on me until I caught up to her, when she remarked in clipped, maidenly tones, "I was just looking at your knees!" Was my face red! However, I don't remember lowering the hem, for you see, I just had to be in fashion.

No Jowels and The Bend Emblem Club

As told by Dutch Stover in 1953 to Kessler Cannon, KBND radio

William D. Cheney started the Bend Emblem Club in 1913 as a way to promote the city. Cheney was a wealthy developer who moved to Bend from Seattle in 1911. He really promoted the Bend area. He had people coming in from all around. Back in Ohio lots were being sold in Bend. That's one of the reasons I came out to Bend in the first place. It was really a nation-wide promotion that he was behind, bringing these people in the way he did. He owned everything from the edge of town to Pilot Butte almost, and north and south as far as the town extended. He had the idea that Bend would be a second Spokane. Cheney was about thirty years before his time. His idea of promotion was really a high class one.

Cheney got together several of Bend's most prominent citizens at a dinner party in the home of George Palmer Putnam. I think Putnam was a member of the Bulletin or part owner. Those men became the founders of the Bend Emblem Club.

The symbol of the Bend Emblem Club was the name Bend made to look like a stained glass circle. You can see it on the windows of the O'Kane Building at the corner of Bond and Oregon Streets. You can also see it in the stained glass window of the original Presbyterian Church at the corner of Franklin and Harriman.

A second emblem associated with the Emblem Club was the honeybee. You can see a honeybee emblem over the O'Kane Building entrance on Oregon Street. Club members were also members of the Order of the Honeybee. The men were the bumblebees and the women were the honeybees. They had their dances once a month and they were formal. When I first came out here I didn't bring any formal clothes with me. And about the first week I was here they said they were going to have a dance at the Emblem Club and did I have my formal clothes. I had to send for them. Everything that he ever did over there was formal.

You didn't pay any dues. Cheney paid for the promotional activities himself. He footed all the bills. I think that perhaps some of the people around town have seen the picture of the thirteen bad men that held up the train. That was a train that came in from Seattle and with all expenses paid by Cheney. The Emblem Club members staged a hold up. Clyde McKay and J.P. Keyes and Ward Coble were part of 'The Great Train Robbery.' They were tough looking guys. They actually stopped the train and made everybody get out. They wore masks and the people really thought that they were being held up. Then they were brought in here and royally entertained by Cheney and taken on tours of land that was being offered for sale just west of Pilot Butte.

George Putnam and Cheney thought up another event, which included the "eruption" of Lava Butte for the benefit of the visiting Portland Ad Club. The year was 1915 or 1916. The idea was to do a take-off on the story of a Joe Knowles who went into the woods with no clothes and lived for a month. Joe Knowles was changed into "No Jowels," and I was selected to be the goat. I was supposed to go out in the woods and live for a month before the Portland Ad Club came to town.

Pictures were taken and published in the Oregonian newspaper prior to the arrival of the Ad Club. The first was when I went out, with just sagebrush around me. I was supposed to get the rubber in the rubber boots I had on from a rubber tree. And I had killed a bear in the meantime, of course, and had the bear's robe on. The silk in the hat that I wore was from a silk worm found in the forest.

Finally the Ad Club members came to town, and everything was set. They took them on the west side of the river to start with, over around Benham Falls. The occasion for stopping at Lava Butte was timed. There was a big sign there that No Jowels would make his appearance that day and within the hour. So just about that time, Lava Butte started erupting. We had put detonators in flour sacks up in the trees. So they went off and this flour was coming down, and some of the men got a little disturbed about it. These fellows asked what that was. We said that Lava Butte had recently shown signs of activity. Then all of a sudden Lava Butte really erupted in earnest.

Burt Roberts was in charge of setting off fireworks up there. That was my cue to come out of the forest leading a tame bear with me. The bear was really Jack Goodell dressed up in a bear suit. Unfortunately, Burt set fire to the whole thing, unintentionally, and he was badly burned and had to be rushed to the hospital. Then after that, the Ad Club members were all brought back to town and given a banquet, which WP Cheney headed and paid for.

Cheney went down to the oil fields in Oklahoma about 1919 but I don't think he ever came back to Bend. The Bend Emblem Club disbanded in 1924. But I've got pictures to remind me of those days and I look at them every once in a while.

They saw opportunities, they saw possibilities
and they didn't dwell on what couldn't be done.

Ken Dramer, Radio Talk Show Host

Bend Athletic Club

Stories of the Flu Epidemic of 1918

As told by J.D. Donovan in 1953 to Kessler Cannon, KBND radio

I recall the flu epidemic of 1918 here in Central Oregon. That flu was a terrible, terrible thing. Thirty-six people died during that epidemic. You'd be feeling all right today, and tomorrow you was down with that flu, they called it the black flu, I think. And of course we had none of these miracle medicines to use at that time. They used mostly quinine and camphorated oil, and stuff like that, which probably today, they'd hang you if you did use it!

Judge Sawyer of the city commission called me in one day about noon, and wanted to know if I could figure out some way to take care of this epidemic. I said, "Yes, if the boys would get back of me, why we would take over the Athletic Club and have something going pretty soon." So we opened up the old Bend Athletic Club[1] to use as an emergency hospital to care for the flu cases. That's the only place where there was room enough to set up. Everybody joined in...they strung wires across through the big building up there, put sheets to separate the beds from each other and made private rooms out of the whole thing - a bed to each section that was set off. And that's the way it was handled.

I had to get out and practice medicine almost like any of the doctors because there was so few doctors here. Dr. Vandevert and Dr. Farrel and the few old doctors what were here just had more than they could do. I remember one preacher that was pretty sick, and they sent for me to come up and see him. We were using moonshine whiskey in some cases! I told this old feller I guessed we'd better get a little something for him to take, and we got him pretty tight on some moonshine...he got over it. Whether that was the thing that cured him or not, I'll never know. That's about all we had to use...camphorated oil, quinine, whiskey...just such drugs as was in common use at the time.

The people that were sick and the people that were getting well were right together there on the floor of the gymnasium. I remember that we'd have people die in that place there, and the undertaker was so busy that he couldn't come up sometimes and get them out. We'd have to keep 'em out someplace in the back there for a few hours while we'd get an undertaker in to take care of them.

We had a boxcar made into a hospital out in Brook's camp, and I made trips out there to kind of help supervise that set up, and we used one of those cabins out in Shevlin's camp. Made a three bed hospital out of that. We didn't have ambulances in those days to bring those that were sick into town. Those that were very bad we'd try to get into the hospital. We had to bring them in the back seat of the car, most any way we could get them in.

I remember once a girl that we had out waiting tables in the camp took sick and I went out to get her; went out in a taxicab. I got out there and started back in with her, and she was in the back seat. The driver said to me, "I believe we lost our patient." I turned around to take a look, and I said, "Wait a minute." She'd slipped off the seat and down behind the front seat. I started to get her back up in the seat and wrap her up a little better to get her in to the hospital, and something got into my hand. I didn't know what it was, but I slipped it in the pocket of my old bearskin overcoat. I thought it was some of her wearing apparel.

After we got into the hospital and turned her over to the nurses, I went home to clean up a little bit. Then the nurse called me and said, "Get over here as soon as you can. This woman's going crazy about what went with her hair!" I said, "What do you mean, her hair?" And she said, "Well, she had a toupee and she lost it." The next morning when I started out on my rounds I put my hand in my overcoat pocket and that thing was there. I brought it down, slipped it to the nurse, and got out before the woman could see me!

We had one big, fine Swedish boy that was living downtown in a boarding house, and they called up and said we should bring him to the hospital, he was pretty sick. We went down to get him, and brought him up in the car and coming up the steps into the hospital he died, right on the steps...right in front of the hospital. That's how fast that stuff worked. It was a terrible thing to see.

Dr. Fobner, a dentist, was in his office one day, and next day he was home sick in bed. Dr. Hendershott went over to see him, was giving him some shots of camphorated oil, and I could see that Dr. Fobner was pretty badly worried. He called me back in when Dr. Hendershott left, and he said, "Do you think I'm going to get well?" I wanted to say, "Why sure, you're going to get well." But I said, "You want to make out some papers or anything like that, I'd attend to it, then you'll feel better." He called in a lawyer and had his papers fixed up and in two hours he was dead.

If there was a good thing about the epidemic it was that the whole community pitched in to help and it was wonderful what the people did. The schools were closed because of the flu and most of the schoolteachers joined in as nurses to help in every way they could. One of the warmest remembrances is of the hearty help given by the community in caring for the patients in the emergency hospital.

I'll always remember Bob Sawyer who came in and worked a shift every day, and Mrs. Paul Hosmer and her sister, who were teaching in the Bend School. There were a lot of the other teachers whose names I don't remember, but I can't forget Mrs. Emerson Stockwell, who handled the diet kitchens for us. Everyone did a wonderful job. No one was ever paid a cent for it, but they had the pleasure and the happiness of knowing they had done a job well.

[1] Site of the current Boy's and Girl's Club

Home Remedies
Excerpted from
As Grandma Used to Say, 'Fort Rock Recollections'
By Lois Boatwright Irby and Roberta Miles

Eat all the onions and garlic you can stand and the smell alone will keep sick people away, plus all the vitamins and sech.

To treat arthuritis:
Honey and whiskey, take according to your needs.

Whiskey soaked brown paper bag on sore spots after reddend with hot packs. Of course some people think fresh cow manure works too.

To treat bruises:
Mix bear grease, goose grease and rattlesnake grease with a good liniment.

To treat coldsores:
Moisten a small amount of horse manure and apply, <u>do not lick lips</u>.

The Lure of the Desert
Helen Varco Brown

Magazines and newspapers seem to have had an influence in my life. It was the advertising in the papers that lured my grandparents and my father to stake a claim on a high desert homestead. And later on, my name Helen was one my folks chose, because they were reading a continued story in a magazine about a girl with that name. But, I'm getting ahead of myself. I'd better start at the beginning.

Granddad and Grandma Bishop, my mother's parents, first moved to Portland so he could open a meat market. Apparently that didn't satisfy him, because when he saw all the advertising about homesteads in the high desert, he and grandma packed up to go out to the Brothers area. Most of that advertising proved to be false in later years, but not before enticing a lot of people way out to that little town named after five sets of brothers that were living there. My mother, Laura Bishop, had stayed in Portland to finish high school before joining her folks on the desert.

My dad was working on a farm that his brother had bought up in Canada when they heard about this place in Oregon where they could "get rich fast." There were 40-acre homesteads available and the farming was supposed to be great, so they headed down here to make their fortune. Once there, he served as the clerk charged with the responsibility of hiring a schoolteacher for the Brothers School. When he heard there was a young girl on the Bishop place, he rode over to find out if that girl, who was my mother, wanted to take the teaching position.

After passing the required test in Prineville, she settled into teaching. She had to ride 24-miles round trip each day to the school. Mother loved horses and she spent all her spare time riding and exploring the country. I often wondered if she hadn't taken the job just so she could ride those 24 miles each day.

When father and mother were getting to know each other, they discovered that they had both come from Michigan and had lived not twenty miles apart! My folks were married in the fall of 1915 and Mother left teaching to work on the homestead. When they needed supplies, she would hitch up the team to the buckboard wagon and head for Bend. When my brother Charles was a baby she would tuck him under the seat of the wagon when she made that trip to Bend. She'd always check from time to time to see how he was doing under her seat. One time she looked down and Charles was gone. She stopped the wagon to search for him and found him lying up against the back of the wagon bed. He must have been an awfully quiet, good baby not to have been hollering.

When I was a little girl I fell against the wood stove one winter and the whole left side of my face was burned. Being worried about it healing up, mother checked with the druggist to see what could be done. He recommended keeping it covered with Ungentine Salve. When it had healed, she wrote the company and told them how success-ful it was in keeping my face from scarring. That company sent her a whole case of the salve, and used her comments in a magazine.

Some of my other fond memories are of my brother Charles's Shetland pony that Granddad gave him for his fifth birthday. Mother still loved messing with horses, and she combined that with her love of parades. She would dress Charles up as Charlie Chaplin and decorate the pony and take us all to the parade. Hauling the pony was no problem; she would just load him in the Model A Coupe between the front and the back seat.

Eventually we left the high desert to get to a less extreme climate as well as to be close to the schools and other things we needed in town. Like so many other families, false advertising lured me to the desert, but reality drove us away.

Helen (Varco) Brown was born in her grandparents' home on Kingston St. in Bend. She attended Redmond schools and worked at Central Oregon District Hospital nearly 20 years. Her father was a County Commissioner for many years and she continues to live in Redmond.

Helen Brown

Horse Packing at Odell Lake
Omar Moffitt

I think our family came here in 1884 or 1885. They homesteaded on Powell Butte. In the summertime we ran a string of packhorses at Cascade Summit over at Odell Lake. We ran little over twenty head of horses. People hired us to get them in the back country.

If you had that many horses, you'd hobble them in a meadow so they could graze. Most of the time, that worked pretty good, but one time the horses took off from us when we were at Charlton Lake. They just left. Guess they didn't like it there. They started towards home. We had a couple of horses staked out, we grabbed them and lit out. It took a half day to herd them back to camp.

At that time there was no road around Odell Lake. There was a road at each end, but you had to go across by boat. That was how folks took up all the stuff for the summer.

It was only summer cabins up there. There weren't any stores around the lakes. At Cascade Summit there was a lodge that sold some things that they brought in on the train but it was expensive. So we brought everything up with us. I remember we had a sixteen-foot rowboat with a motor on it that we'd load close to the waterline taking stuff to the cabin.

Folks would come up there and we'd take 'em out. The greatest trip I ever went on was with Dr. Bob Hemmingway, his wife and the McDougals from Chicago. They went on a two-week pack trip from Odell to Elk Lake. Dad hired Glen Ritter to do the cookin'. He was a real camp cook making baking powder biscuits in a cast iron dutch oven and all. The doctors really liked it. We went to Salmon Lake, west and a little north of Waldo Lake.

Hauling the doctors out to camp was a big production. We packed one horse completely with booze. They never drank very much; they just didn't want to run out.

I got to fish all the time. There were quite a few fish then and easy to catch. Glen would smoke 'em, and it was great. Dad and I would ride out to some of those little lakes around to see how they were for fishin'. We went over to a lake on the other side of Waldo Mountain. I put my pole together and in fifteen minutes I caught four good-sized ones. Those fish were fighters too. The doctors saw me pulling those fish in and they couldn't hardly catch a fish.

We had an old horse that was loco. You never knew when she'd buck. You could ride all day, then out of the blue, she'd buck. And I'd be underneath her lookin' up. And she looked back at me as if to say, "What are you doin' down there?"

There was a young fellow that was older than I was and he was wantin' a horse. So we told him that this horse was a good horse. She gets a little loco once in a while, which didn't hurt you, but she just might buck yah off. It didn't seem to worry him so I traded the horse for his bicycle. I don't know if he ever got bucked off. He never said.

But he bred that horse and got a good colt, and he kept horses all his life. And I kept the bicycle.

Omar Moffitt, b. 1923 in Prineville, Oregon. He lived in Brothers and Millican areas raising sheep and cattle. He traveled extensively in the Northwest shearing sheep and marketed wool to the Pendleton Wool Company. He currently lives in Redmond.

Read All About It .... Redmond's Gold Strike!
Excerpted from a Martha Stranahan article in the Redmond Spokesman

Redmond was the City of Golden Dreams as the year 1915 unfolded.

"The largest gold-producing fields in the world . . . richest ever known . . ." were predicted for the Redmond area in January, 1915 as assays of sands from the Deschutes and Crooked Rivers and Squaw Creek indicated they might contain gold and other valuable mineral deposits.

The Redmond Spokesman of Jan. 28, 1915 reported a Portland mining engineer and his attorney, C. W. Clapp and Will Bard, were in Redmond by invitation of local businessmen, William M. Wilson and Guy E. Dobson, to gather ore samples at Cline Falls for assay in Portland. From his on-site eyeball appraisal the engineer opined "the volcanic ash and sand in the vicinity of Redmond contained gold, silver, platinum, iridium, uranium and iron..."

A Seattle and Alaska mining authority George E. Baldwin, stressed that hundreds of samples must be assayed to establish certainty of pay dirt, but he felt confident enough to invest money here.

Reportedly, in the Feb. 18 issue, "gold mining experts from all over the world" had been in Redmond and believed the Redmond Gold District to be the "largest and will be the most productive ever known to man." The rumors of gold prompted a hustle to file mining claims, and promising sites were being investigated all around Redmond and into Jefferson County. Samples from Grey Butte and Bear Creek were "running rich in gold and other minerals."

Gold prospectors reported good finds and recalled that relatives had panned in the area 20 years previously. Portlanders leased the "Escondido" mine site and 10 other gold quartz claims were filed in February, 1915 with the "biggest strike" yet reported on the Metolius River, filed upon by 27 Redmond men.

Bard reported construction underway of a demonstration mill at Lower Bridge and promised to buy materials from Redmond merchants. It was predicted several mills would be in operation by snow time. By August gold filings were reported on nearly 6,000 acres along Squaw Creek. The August 19, 1915 Spokesman predicted the mill will be "turning out gold" by Sept. 1. To doubters, the paper urged . . . "try anything once."

On Nov. 4, 1915 the paper declared "gold values are here in untold quantities," citing Bard's optimism.

February, 1916 showed continued interest in gold mills, a new one at Cline Falls, and the existing mill at Lower Bridge.

News of gold fades in the news before war, wheat, potatoes, dairying, roads, land policy, irrigation water, the banks, newspaper, and merchants of the Redmond area.

The Spokesman for June 29, 1916 quotes the Portland Oregonian— "Redmond is all right. The town is not on 'the boom' but has settled down to a substantial basis. No doubt the place will gain in pace with the advancement of the tributary country. If it does, it will always be a good town and eventually a large one, for the farmers thereabouts are bound to gain rapidly in prosperity!"

Was Redmond's gold, after all, in the hearts and endeavors of its people and not in the river and desert sands?

Martha Stranahan was born in Pittsburgh, Pennsylvania. She graduated from Westminster College with a degree in English and Journalism. She came west with her husband and moved to Oregon in 1945 and worked as a free-lance writer for 40 years. She now lives with "Indy," her Dachshund dog.

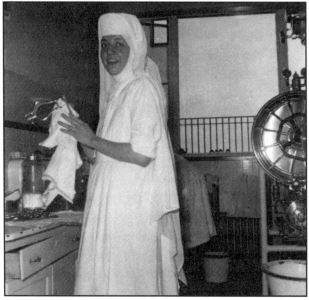

Sister Catherine, 1949

Taking Care of Everyone

Sister Catherine Hellmann

The Sisters of St. Joseph of Tipton, Indiana took over the operation of the Emergency Hospital in Bend in 1918. The small fourteen-bed hospital was located where the Mirror Pond parking lot is now. It was built for the mill workers. J. D. Donovan, who operated the hospital, advised the Sisters to take care of only mill employees. The Sisters would not agree to that. They wanted to care for everyone in need of medical attention. How the Sisters from Tipton came to Bend is a story worth retelling.

When Father Luke Sheehan of the Catholic Church was returning to Ireland in 1908, he met Mother Gertrude, founder of the Sisters of St Joseph, on the boat. Father Sheehan asked Mother Gertrude if the Sisters could come to Bend. She said they couldn't honor his request because they did not have enough nurses and they were a teaching order. In 1915, Father Sheehan wrote to Mother Gertrude and again asked their assistance in providing hospital services. Again she said, "I'm so sorry but we don't have the nurses."

The next year his request was denied again. In 1917, he asked Bishop Charles O'Reilly, if he could go to Indiana and beg Mother Gertrude one more time. Father Sheehan went to see Mother Gertrude who was battling cancer. He told her that people were dying and pleaded with her to just send three Sister nurses. She agreed, and though she died, her commitment was honored.

Three Sister nurses and two other nuns volunteered to go 2,000 miles West knowing they would never get back home. On Christmas day, 1917, the five nuns boarded the train with their little suitcases. They had no money to pay their train fare, but were given passes. Father Sheehan met them in Pendleton and brought them to Bend. He took all the Sisters to his own parish house, which the priests had vacated, for the Sisters' temporary home. On January 1, 1918, they signed the contract and took over management of the Emergency Hospital, stating they would serve everyone.

The Sisters expanded the hospital from 14 to 28 beds. In 1920 the Catholic Church purchased Hospital Hill in downtown Bend and donated it to the Sisters for the construction of a new hospital named St. Charles after Bishop Charles O'Reilly. Two years later, the Sisters moved into a new 30-bed brick structure on Hospital Hill.

In the new hospital, the nuns slept in the elevator pit so they would be available to the patients at all times. The patients knocked on the door if they needed something. Bishop O'Reilly didn't like them sleeping there so they built a dorm-type room behind the hospital. Six-foot walls divided the room into spaces big enough for a bed and dresser.

The Sisters found the people and culture of Bend a bit different, but they were so open to new things. The residents of Bend were very helpful to them. They brought the Sisters food and paid their bills with a half of beef, a crate of chickens or a couple dozen eggs.

The nuns never received a salary. We were supposed to send seven dollars a month for each Sister back to the Mother House. For years we didn't have the seven dollars to send, because we were still being paid with chickens and eggs. Once after a late night surgery, I was hungry. I thought I'd go to the kitchen and get a donut before I went to bed. I was sorry I did because the other nuns were there with two crates of chickens and they asked me to help pluck 'em. It was 2:00 a.m. before we finished. It wasn't until Medicare that the Sisters were paid a salary, which was sent back to the Mother House.

Wednesdays were supposed to be the nuns' day off in honor of St. Joseph's day, but very seldom did we actually get it. When we did, we wanted to climb the mountains, but how can you climb a mountain wearing a habit? Our solution was to pin up our skirts and wear an old pair of slacks under the habit. When word reached the Mother House that we'd climbed mountains wearing slacks, they were shocked that those nuns out West were wearing slacks with their habits on!

I know we did other things that would have shocked them too. The brick hospital had a fire chute. In case of fire, the patients were put on a mattress and slid down it. One winter evening, Sister Ruth and I decided that instead of going to the recreation hour with the older nuns we would give it a try. So we got granite bedpans, sat on them and slid down that chute which was covered with ice and snow. Sister Ruth almost hit a tree and I did smack my arm. I couldn't get a x-ray because I would have had to tell what we had done.

The Sisters stayed around the clock if necessary. They would lay a blanket on the floor in the room and rest. Once I was riding a bus to Portland when a man told me his name was Charles Edward. He said he was born in Bend. The doctor didn't expect him or his mother to live. However, Sister Edward stayed right in the room with them day and night rendering care and compassion. They both pulled through. He was named Charles after St. Charles and Edward after Sister Edward.

In the 40's we had a polio epidemic. The patients were put in iron lungs to keep them breathing. The City paid my way to Colorado to study treating patients in iron lungs. We were put in the iron lung so we would know what the patient was feeling. I never forgot my pain in the iron lung and thinking about those patients I was helping.

The City of Bend will never forget Sister Catherine. Under her guiding hand, St. Charles became a first-rate medical center where the spirit of those founding Sisters lives on.

Sister Catherine Hellmann came to Bend in 1948 as a nurse with the Sisters of St. Joseph. She returned to nursing in Indiana in 1951, the day after dedicating the new building on Hospital Hill. She came back to St. Charles in 1969 as the hospital administrator. She has continued to serve in hospital administration since then and is currently President Emeritus.

St Charles Memorial Hospital
Lava Road Facilities 1918-1975

Service to Our Neighbors

Lowell Jensen

From a panel discussion moderated by Paul Reynolds on April 25, 2000

Of course, my big pet was St. Charles Hospital, which was started by the Sisters of St. Joseph's in 1918. They came to Bend at the request of Father Luke Sheehan. Initially they operated a twelve-bed hospital, but as Bend grew so did its need for hospital beds.

The idea was to build a new hospital adjacent to the old building on Hospital Hill (current location of the Phoenix Inn). The problem was, the Sisters didn't have any money. They'd never made any running the hospital, so they asked the Chamber of Commerce if they couldn't do something to help. Carl Johnson was a member on the Chamber of Commerce and he called in the State Board of Health. At that time there was a lot of bigotry in town and some strong feelings about Catholics. The truth is, there were a lot of people that wanted a hospital, but they didn't want the Catholics to run it.

When the State Board of Health came to town to evaluate our need, they went through the old hospital and talked to the Sisters. Then they told us, "We'll go for an enlargement of the present hospital, but we won't go for a new hospital to go in competition with those nuns, because if you do, you'll go broke. They're working for nothing."

So the Chamber called a meeting of the entire city of Bend up at the old Pilot Butte Inn. Carl Johnson presented the need for a professional fund drive to raise money for the hospital. It was launched and they raised $323,000. That was quite a lot of money at that time, but it was just a starter for a hospital. They figured their new hospital on the hill would cost $1 million.

The Hill Burton funds supplied a third of that, but the Sisters couldn't have a mortgage on the hospital. That meant they had to raise two-thirds in Bend. We were supposed to have worked two weeks on this professional fund drive, but three months later we were still at it and we still didn't have a hospital. Then one day Carl Johnson came to our morning meeting and said, "I've got news for you. The Sisters can borrow $200,000 on a note." Well, that was the encouragement we needed to keep going. We finally raised the money and they built the hospital up on the hill.

When Sister Blanche cut the ribbon in 1951 she said that the St. Charles Medical Center doors will never be locked against anyone. "The only reason for our presence in your midst is service," she added. "Service to our neighbors and through them to our God." Alva Goodrich, who was on the Board at that time was heard to say, "Now those are words that are going to stay with St. Charles as long as there is a St. Charles."

The Sisters hired Bill Stolmack as Manager of the hospital and he was a good one. According to Alva Goodrich, Bill said that it was the only hospital that was built by the Protestants, run by the Catholics and managed by a Jew!

Hardy Myers, the manager of the Shevlin-Hixon Company was on our board as well as Morris Hitchcock who had Bend Wholesale Hardware. We sent those two men up to see Sister Blanche and find out what the hospital had done in the last seven or eight years. We met at 7 o'clock every morning at the Pilot Butte Inn Coffee Shop. They reported on two mornings.

On the third morning, Hardy Myers came through the door, hit the desk and said, "By God, I don't know how that woman's kept those doors open. It's the people down on Wall Street that owe her the money. Let's take over the finances of that hospital and let them do the nursing." Well, they presented that to Sister Blanche and she was delighted. "Now," she said, "we can do what we were sent out here to do; nurse the sick." So, we took over and everything has been going pretty good since then.

Lowell Jensen, b. 1907 in Idaho, came to the Bend area in 1923 at age 18. He owned a gas and oil distributing business and was active in civic affairs. For 35 years he has been a faithful visitor to people in retirement and nursing homes.

(L) Maren Gribskov (R) Martha Becher

Bend's Favorite Cook and Restaurateur

As told by Maren Gribskov to Shirley Ray

In the summer of 1919, two recent graduates of Oregon Agricultural College, Maren Gribskov and Martha Bechen traveled throughout the state in a newly acquired touring car searching for a place to start a restaurant.

They chose Bend after observing that it had a large population of bachelors that had come to work in the mills, many of the local teachers needed a place to eat and, perhaps most important, the payroll was substantial for a small town.

Martha and Maren found an old, dilapidated restaurant available on Bond Street across from Aune's livery stable. The interior was very dirty, but the girls scrubbed, painted, and discarded old dishes and equipment. They sewed new curtains and table-cloths, purchased new dishes, pots and pans. There was a wood range for cooking with a hot water tank attached. Electric lights were available, as well as one restroom. Lunch was to be the main meal and everything was to be served cafeteria style, a novelty to most of the customers who soon enjoyed choosing the items they preferred. Martha and Maren did all the cooking, cleaning, shopping and serving. It was named O.I.C. Cafeteria. They had trouble deciding on an appropriate name and settled on initials that said: "Oh, I see" a place to eat.

39

The O.I.C.'s opening day was September 9, 1919. It was a wonder that they managed to survive their first winter in Bend for that was the year of the "blue snow." When telling about it years later Maren said, "There was about 52" of snow in town for four miserable weeks. We were absolutely marooned from the outside world - no mail and no produce because the trains couldn't get in. As the snow melted the roof leaked and the plumbing froze."

The time came when it was appropriate to hire their first employee. One applicant was questioned closely. She seemed qualified, but her hair was bobbed! In spite of this questionable trait the woman was hired and remained with them for years.

Maren's parents were Danish immigrants who were farming in Junction City, Oregon. During the early years, Maren's mother raised and dressed chickens and produced eggs for the restaurant. These were shipped to Bend by train and purchased by the girls at prevailing prices.

After two years on Bond Street the cafeteria was moved to a building on Wall, where it remained for several years. It was located in what was later called the Wetle Building, where Wetle Way is now. In 1928 Martha married Sid Conklin and went with him into the mill camps, leaving Maren to operate the restaurant.

Maren had been admiring a piece of property on the river for some time, feeling it would be a lovely setting for a restaurant. She formed a new partnership with Eleanor Bechen, Martha's sister. They pooled their resources, somehow convinced bankers that they were a good risk, borrowed what they could and, in spite of the Depression, built the Pine Tavern. It opened just before Christmas in December of 1936. Throughout the years of ownership the building and land were a joint partnership, but the restaurant operation was Maren's.

Financially it was nip-and-tuck for awhile, but with good food, good service and a friendly atmosphere, the residents in town rallied around. The business not only survived but also built a reputation as the best eating place in Bend. During World War II Camp Abbott soldiers and their families filled the place to capacity and many of the service wives became temporary employees.

The service clubs met there weekly: Kiwanis, Lions, 20-30 Club which became the Jaycees, and others. After the demise of the Pilot Butte Inn, the Pine Tavern catered all the major conventions that came to Bend. Ladies luncheons, wedding receptions, company Christmas parties; receptions for new teachers and wives of new doctors were some of the events which were scheduled. Many locals still remember the Saturday night Smorgasbords that were served during the 40s, 50s and 60s.

For many years the O.I.C. Cafeteria and Pine Tavern were about the only places of employment for "respectable" women and girls of Bend. Summers found Bend's college girls making up a good share of the staff, many returning each summer until graduation. A majority of the permanent employees were just that - permanent - staying 10, 20 and even 40 years. With the exception of an occasional family member, no men were employed until sometime during the 50s.

Being acknowledged as Bend's Senior Citizen in 1967 was certainly appropriate. It was the first time a woman was chosen for that honor. In addition to placing Bend on the map with good food and service, she had been active in the community and had invested in almost every new business selling stock - from the pencil factory to a trailer manufacturer and a toy plane company - but Mt. Bachelor was the successful one.

In 1959, with the collaboration of Eileen Donaldson, the Pine Tavern Cookbook was published and there have been many reprints. The Pine Tavern was sold on December 1, 1967.

Maren Gribskov passed away on July 16, 1984, one month after her 90th birthday. She had lived 65 years in a town she loved. The citizens of Bend returned her affection and loved the woman who kept them well fed.

Shirley (Gribskov) Ray, b. 1926 in Junction City, Oregon. As a child, she lived with her Aunt Maren Gribskov above the Pine Tavern during the summers. She later worked as her aunt's assistant at the restaurant for many years.

Marjorie B Smith

The View From 935 Wall Street
Marjorie B. Smith

My dad, N.P. Smith, a timber cruiser and surveyor, was one of the early settlers in Central Oregon. He came here from Bemidji, Minnesota with his wife, Cora. They first homesteaded in Tumalo, later moving into a house in what is now Pioneer Park down by the Deschutes River, and then to one on Hawthorne Street, and finally to an apartment over the store on Wall. In 1903 there were only 286 people living in Bend.

I was the first baby born in the first Bend Hospital. It was located on Oregon Avenue where the parking lot next to the downtown post office is now. One of my brothers was born in Wasco County, another in Crook County, and I in Deschutes.

Dad opened a hardware store on the east side of Wall Street. Later, around 1909, the present building at 935 Wall Street was built. His store was on the ground floor and the family lived upstairs. Those days lots of the folks who had businesses in town lived above their stores. Our proximity to the store sure made it handy for Mom to call Dad to dinner. All she had to do was pound on the floor with a broom handle and he'd come running. While he ate, one of the family members would mind the store.

I remember, as a child half-playing and half-working in the store, particularly playing in the nail bins and mixing them up. But my dad never got angry when he'd discover the wrong nails in the wrong bins. It was also fun to hide in the rope room. It was in the back of the store. I'd hide and peek out the holes in the wall where the rope was pulled through and measured off.

It's the only original wooden building today in the business district on Wall Street. It's even on the Historic Register. The other buildings in the area were destroyed in a fire, but Mom and Dad saved that building by draping wet bedding all over it. From our apartment you could see all the way across the river. In those days there was just the river with trees on the west side of Wall Street. It was a beautiful view.

My dad helped build a mountain lodge for A.M. Drake on the east side of the Deschutes River where the Mirror Pond parking lot is now. Dad built a long rock wall from the Drake home to Wall Street. It really dominated the view in the early days and it's that wall that gave Wall Street its name.

Dad also helped to clear tree stumps from the roadside on Wall Street. And he helped build the wooden sidewalks. The sidewalks were raised above the roadway so it'd be easier to walk and not be in the dirt and mud and snow.

Bend was a good town to grow up in. My two brothers and I had lots of kids to play with. Most of the activity centered about the home. We girls learned to embroider, crochet, and knit. My brothers used to spend a lot of time riding their bikes. They never let me ride because they said I was too young, so I never learned how. I remember, in the wintertime we went sledding on what is now Portland Avenue. We would sled right down the middle of the street, but there were hardly any cars to worry about back then.

We always celebrated birthdays. My brothers would ask for chocolate cake with chocolate icing. Not me. I wanted a three-layer cake - white, strawberry, and chocolate. And each year the frosting would be chosen from one of those three flavors. There were so many kids around, it seemed like we were always going to someone's birthday party.

Christmas was also a special time. We would get a big tree and decorate it. The churches had celebrations and the families would all bring some food to share. Back then there were three churches in town that are still in the same location today - the Methodist, Baptist, and Episcopal.

On family vacations we would go huckleberry picking at Hog Rock and fishing in the lakes throughout the area. Dad sold fishing tackle in the store, so naturally he had to try out the different lures and rods and all. He'd go up to the lakes to fish and then he could tell his customers what to buy. I think he really enjoyed that business.

On one of those fishing trips, Mom was riding with him in the car and she said, "I want Marjorie to learn to drive." Since she didn't know how to drive, she thought that in an emergency it was necessary for me to know how. Well, Dad said, "No girl of mine is going to drive a car." Mom opened the car door and said, "Then I'm getting out!" Dad was afraid she would get hurt, so he agreed to teach me to drive. As I remember, he was a very patient teacher too.

I began school in Reid School, which now houses the Deschutes Historical Museum. Later I went to the junior high school, which was the wooden building near the old brick high school on Lafayette Street. In my junior year we moved into the new high school which is now the Bend-LaPine School District Administration Building. I enjoyed playing basketball in the old gym, which is now the Boys and Girls Club. We played tennis on an outdoor court, which is now the Kenwood School playground. As teenagers, we went to football games on Bruin Field, which is where BiMart is now. As you can see, nothing is as it was before.

I still live in the apartment where I grew up, but I miss the close-knit community we once had when everything was downtown. The view from my window has changed so much. Sometimes it seems that only my memories and the mountains are the same today as they were yesterday.

Marjorie B. Smith was the first baby born in the first hospital in Bend - September 14, 1909. She has lived in Bend most of her life on the family property in the 900 block of Wall Street. She had a long career in teaching and has been honored as the Pioneer Queen and Grand Marshall of the Christmas Parade.

Two Big Fires in Bend

As told by Lloyd S.Blakely in 1953 to Kessler Cannon, KBND radio

In 1912, my father worked for Brooks-Scanlon Lumber Company in Louisiana. He came to Bend to work in the small western mill they owned called the Bend Company. From 1916 until he passed away in 1943, he was the logging superintendent.

Long about 1915 or 1916, the mill caught fire by the Tumalo Avenue Bridge. I was still a kid living on Greenwood Avenue. I was looking out the door, watching Elmer Ward delivering big blocks of ice for everyone's iceboxes, when I looked up to see a huge billowing cloud of smoke rising up.

Mother and I headed on over towards the fire. As we got down near the Tumalo Bridge, we saw an old model car lurching down the gravel street pulling the hose cart. The cart bounced and bucked off the bumper taking off through the grass down by where the park is now. After it careened to a stop, the throng of men that were milling around ran up to the cart and grabbed it. Pulling and pushing, they hauled it the rest of the way to the fire.

There was a volunteer fire department and running water, but there wasn't any pressure. The water tank was on top of Hospital Hill and the gravity flow just didn't make for a very powerful stream of water.

That blaze torched the entire lumberyard, spewing sparks and black smoke. The only thing the men could save was the sawmill, There wasn't much use for that with the lumber burned up. The force of the fire was so intense that charred boards scattered out to Pilot Butte.

There was also the big fire on Bond Street before Prohibition. Just about every business on Bond Street was a saloon or honky tonk. The frame structures were like torches and that whole block of saloons burned to the ground. The men panicked because they were afraid the whiskey would be lost. They rushed into the buildings to get the liquor. Everyone was hustling to keep the hooch safe. They did a pretty good job the first few trips. The trouble was the men kept tipping the bottles to fortify themselves. After several trips, they got a little too tipsy to take the mission seriously. They had a swell time trying though.

THE WANDERING TOWN
OF SHEVLIN

Logging Camp Life - First View

Mary Mihelchich

I got married in 1931 when I was seventeen and we moved to the Shevlin logging camp about 3 miles from LaPine. There were 700 - 800 families living in that one big group. That was our honeymoon, from my mom's to the camp!

We rented a two-room house - a kitchen and a bedroom. That was big enough for two, you know, until we started getting a family. Then they built on a big long part, it was like another bedroom and a family room, and raised our rent from $5 to $10.

We heated every drop of hot water on the stove. There was a little wooden sink, but you had to dump the water out the door. On the porch we had a little cooler for our milk and butter and stuff. When it was cold it was fine. We had to build root cellars to save all our food and keep it as cold as possible other times.

Those little houses were comfortable. We had wood floors and we scrubbed 'em with a broom and light water. I kept everything neat as a pin. Once a month we cleaned the cupboards; we'd take everything out and put in nice fancy paper. The whole camp teased us because we were so clean, but we had time.

Oh, we didn't have lights. We just had kerosene. Every day we'd clean that darn chimney and get it goin'. Water we brought in by buckets. There'd be a faucet way off there and we carried it back. When I got my first washin' machine I didn't even want one. I wore out a metal washboard and thought I did real good by hand.

Monday we'd wash clothes. Tuesday we'd iron. We ironed everything; we ironed our underwear, we ironed the guy's socks, we just did everything that went through the laundry. I don't know why; we were so dumb! And in the wintertime we'd take the clothes and just pinch 'em on the clothesline. Didn't need clothespins cuz they froze just as fast as the air hit 'em.

Wednesday us ladies would get together and crochet or embroider and gossip. And every Friday, I'd go have my hair all pinned. Friday night we'd come to town and stay over 'til Sunday. We stayed with my folks. We'd go to Penney's and the guys'd go to the tavern. I'd go by the tavern and he was havin' a good time and he didn't want to come out.

We didn't have gardens but we had chickens in a little pen. Charlie and John and the gang got together and built a smokehouse. We'd make our own smoked ham and kielbasas and bacon. Boy were they good. We even made blood sausage where you put in corn meal, garlic, and I don't know what all. We never wasted a thing.

We'd cook the old-fashioned way, stews and soups, sauerkraut. We made beer and we made homemade wine. That beer had that thick foam from the barley and it was good stuff. It didn't last us very long.The guys would play and drink, you know. Us girls kept washin' bottles and getting ready for another batch. We'd put the boiler on the stove and fill it with water and then we'd make the beer in that. Then we'd put it behind the stove to ferment for 2, 3 days. When the yeast'd foam up it was ready. We kept it cold in the root cellar before we got refrigerators.

We were in camps 12 years, right into the war. When the logging was done, they'd put all those little bungalows on the boxcars and took 'em to the next camp. Life went on the way it had before but in a new spot.

Mary (Matich) Mihelchich was born in 1914 and came to Central Oregon in 1923 from Utah. She and her husband, John, lived in the Shevlin-Hixon logging camps in the Bend and LaPine area until 1942. She devoted her life to her family and now lives in Bend.

Always There Was the Land

Martha Stranahan, exerpted from the Central Oregon <u>Ruralite</u>,1964

Brothers John and George Bradetich each have had two great love affairs in their lives - one with their beloved wives, and the other with the land they have cultivated.

John came to the United States from Austria in 1910. U.S. Immigration authorities disapproved of people coming here with an open intent to work. So John came to "visit" an uncle. George came in 1913 to "visit" John. Their father, a modest farmer, had died of a snakebite, leaving their young mother with five children. John, then 18, got work in a Portland lumber camp; George was 15 when he joined him.

They didn't fall in love with their future Central Oregon home as fast as they had with the girls who waited for them in the home-land. But after two short tours of work in this area, on Tumalo reservoir construction and for Shevlin-Hixon mill, they elected to ignore desert winds and accept the promise of the Bend region.

By 1919 they had bought 800 acres in a two mile strip east of Bend and south of the landmark Pilot Butte. There the industrious Bradetichs commenced their farming saga, establishing the first grade A dairy in Central Oregon. They bought registered bulls from Weiser, Idaho. The dairy launched and homes a-building; the men summoned their fiancees. On July 24, 1921, John married Mary Rabak and George married Helen Zlatich in the first double wedding service held in St. Francis Church, Bend. (Twenty-eight years later, on November 12, 1949, George's son, Phil, and Dorothy Bush of Bend, and John's daughter, Betty, and Leonard Slate of Bend had a double ceremony in the same church.)

Mary and Helen were as industrious, frugal, forward looking, cheerful, and hopeful as their husbands. And the Bradetich enter-prises prospered. John and Mary had daughters Helen, Edith and Betty. And George and Helen had Phil and Joe.

By 1942, the Bradetichs were milking 105 Holstein and Jersey cows and were ready to make some changes. They sold the dairy and stock and bought land nine miles east of Bend. They eventually built three family residences, two homes for employees and a huge modern shop and storage quonset. Bradetich Brothers Dairy became Pine Mountain Angus Farm. Raising beef cattle permitted more flexibility in their time schedule, although the families continued to work hard.

They removed rocks, sagebrush and junipers from their new acres and began to grow hay and grass for their cattle, and choice Deschutes Russet potatoes for sale and for themselves. For several years they raised certified seed.

The Bradetichs were the first in Deschutes County to initiate aerial chemical sagebrush control. This range improvement plus soil conservation projects earned them the 1953 County Grassman of the Year Award and then the Tri-State (Oregon, Washington, Idaho) Trophy. For the latter award celebration the honorees (now including Phil who entered the partnership in 1952), their families and a busload of friends from the county traveled to Portland. In 1951 they received the Deschutes County Cattleman of the Year trophy. In 1957 they took State champion trophy for potatoes at the Merrill, Oregon show, and the next year had best spuds entered in the Redmond Potato Festival.

They constructed one of the first irrigation, stock water, and trout ponds in the county. It is a nine-acre 'pond'. Cattle are watered at troughs served by the pond. Dorothy Bradetich claims the record trout catch: a 28-inch eight-pounder. She, incidentally, keeps the extensive farm records, and at calving time must name the registered babies — more than a hundred a year!

The Bradetichs finish every head of cattle they raise, marketing in Portland where their beef consistently grades choice or premium, says John. The farm has been visited by farm specialists from many countries, touring county agents, conservationists, irrigationists, politicians, reporters, and neighboring farmers through the years. The hospitable Bradetiches have been proud to show it and to share their farming methods and philosophy.

Energy, imagination, initiative and business acumen, close family ties plus boundless hospitality and friendliness have earned solid respect and admiration for the Bradetichs. The "girls" are gone and for the Bradetich brothers things have certainly changed; but it's spring, and there still is the land.

"Just before I was born, a bigger home was built on the dairy farm. Many people told me what a big mansion I lived in. But the farm and its large house were anything but a mansion. The farm represented long hours of washing bottles and doing many other chores that come with a full service dairy. There was not much time for a social life except for the many visitors that came to the dairy. The 'mansion' was really like a boarding house as many bachelor immigrants would pass through and stay a few days, working a bit and moving on."

Betty Bradetich Slate

Betty (Bradetich) Slate, b. 1930 in Bend, Oregon. She grew up on the family dairy farm east of Bend and attended Richardson grade school (Hamby & Ward Roads). She worked as a telephone operator.

June 16, 1936

Growing Up On The Farm
Violet Klobas Shepard

Every child likes to know what his or her father does in the way of work. On the farm there was never any doubt what your father did. My dad was a farmer in every sense of the word. He made things grow.

We lived two miles east of Bend on Denser Road, 1/4 mile north of the Bend-Burns Highway. From the kitchen window we could see Pilot Butte. On this 40-acre parcel of ground there were many, many rocks and rock piles making the fields quite small. The sandy soil, however, grew most anything once water and fertilizer were added.

Dad tilled the soil manually for many years with a foot-burner plow. He cleared brush, hauled off rocks, plowed, spring-toothed, and leveled the fields with a stump-boat. After planting alfalfa or grain, he would make corrugations to carry the water down the rows. The water came from an irrigation ditch and sod was used to intercept the water. When the water was running properly, all the corrugations would be running evenly. However, many times in this sandy soil, the water would run amuck creating a washout. In new seeding, this could be catastrophic. Therefore, either my dad or one of us would stay in the field, literally sitting with the water to avoid that problem.

There were a wide variety of crops raised on the farm including alfalfa, vetch, clover, wheat, barley, rye, sugar beets and potatoes. Potatoes were considered the cash crop, providing money to pay taxes and to purchase next years seed and fertilizer. If the potatoes froze or the price was low, money would be scarce. Most of the crops raised were to feed the milk cows and beef stock, chicken, pigs, horses...and even a goat or sheep, not to mention the family.

During the 30s, 40s and 50s we milked between eight and fifteen cows. In 1948 we got a milking machine. Since we did not have Grade A facilities, the milk was separated by a machine - first a hand-cranked one and then an electric gadget - which would allow the milk to flow through disks which separated the cream from the skim milk. The skim milk would run through one pipe and the cream down another into their respective containers. We took the cream to the Bend Dairy where it was made into butter. The sale of that cream provided cash every two weeks to buy groceries, chicken feed and occasionally a pair of shoes.

Starting at an early age, one of my jobs was to wash the milk separator machine disks. Now on the surface this would seem like a simple task, but it wasn't. Each of the disks was numbered. Milk solids would adhere to the disks. Each one had to be washed separately and scoured with a stainless steel scouring pad, rinsed, dried and stacked in exact order. If even one was out of place, the cream would not separate out!

We butchered our own chicken, beef, and pork. The meat would be cut up, farmer style, and Mom and I would double wrap it in freezer paper. Then we would take it to Mid-State Meat, next to the Bend Dairy, where it was stored in rented freezer boxes. When someone went to town for groceries they would bring home a package or two of meat. About 1950, we bought a chest-style freezer, which Mom used until 1974.

In the early years of my life, going to town was a real treat and something I looked forward to. We would drop off the cream at the dairy, go to Boise Aune's feed store to get feed and then to the grocery store. My mom would make out a shopping list and by the time I was seven, I would help Dad read it. My mother did not drive and rarely went shopping. This was her time, so to speak, to catch her breath, so I learned shopping skills and price comparisons at a very early age.

There were many foods we enjoyed during my years on the farm. Some included sweet rolls, walnut roll (also called poteca), fatigman (a fried pastry), apple strudel, Holiday Steamed Carrot Pudding with Lemon Sauce, sugar cookies and jelly rolls, just to mention a few.

There was something we had only at Christmas time, usually two days before the holiday, and that was Lutefisk, which is dried, salted cod fish. It had to be soaked at least overnight, and preferably several days, in cold water. The water had to be changed several times and the fish had to be thoroughly washed. This was usually done outside because of the foul odor. Then it was cooked in a large amount of water, also outside, until the fish fell apart. This took several hours and the odor traveled a great distance. There was no doubt what was being cooked when you had Lutefisk on the stove! The fish was mashed with a potato masher until it was quite fine, similar to making tuna sandwich filling. Sautéed garlic was added to the fish along with salt and pepper. It is a very rich dish and is usually served with polenta, a stiff cooked cornmeal, and red wine.

When my husband Jerry was dating me, he happened to be there the day we were serving this for supper. Of course I had to introduce Jerry to our family traditions! This almost became a short courtship! These flavors and flavor combinations did not appeal to him. As with many food customs, this is something that must be part of your heritage so that it might grow on you. Needless to say, this has not been served in our house during these past 40 years, however, I can still smell the smells and taste the flavor!

Violet (Klobas) Shepard was born on the family farm in Bend in 1935. She has been active in 4-H throughout her life and served as a county extension agent.

Boxcar School Days
Alice Bishop

From the time I was five years old in 1919 until 1926, we lived in the timber camps. First the one at Lava Butte Lumber Camp, then Bessie Butte Lumber Camp and finally we moved up to Rocky Top Butte Lumber Camp, which is about five or six miles southeast of Lava Butte.

Oh, life out there was fun. There were probably twelve or fifteen kids. We played a lot of games like Anti Anti Over, where you throw a ball over the house and then run around and try to get there first to catch it before it hits the ground. We played Pump-Pump-Pull Away, though now I can't even remember how it went. It was fun to run around in the woods and pick flowers too. If the men were cutting timber close to camp, we would go out and watch them log the trees. People today would have a fit about that because of the danger, but we didn't think about it bein' dangerous because the men always yelled "Timber" before they felled the trees. We were always back the distance of a tree or farther. And we also knew enough to look and be safe and to run if necessary.

There was an ice cave over by Lava Butte that's covered by the highway now. But when we lived at Lava Butte, around 1920, we'd take a child's wagon and go up to the ice cave and get ice and make homemade ice cream. We'd make it with milk and eggs and vanilla. Of course, it wouldn't keep too long, so we had to eat the whole thing!

The first five years of my schooling were in a school boxcar on the railroad track. They ran a spur off to the side and put the school-house on it. Those cars had windows down one side and two rooms. There was a small one where we put our coats and lunch-boxes and things like that, while the teacher and the pupils were in the other room. Our teacher was always a woman and she taught from ten to twelve students in eight grades in the one box-car. Sometimes there were only one or two children in a class. I know, in my first grade class, there was only one other with me. But that's the way it was.

School was very interesting. The young children would learn from the reports of the older students and we did very well. Every Friday we would have a program. We would sing, recite poetry, and have a math match at the black board. You know, do long division, addition, or fractions or something like that. See who could be first to get through. All the children would do it together. There were spelling bees too. We'd do our recitations and read our stories at her desk. Each class would come up and do their recitals for about 20 minutes. When somebody else was up at her desk, we were supposed to be studying. But I loved to listen to them. So in first grade I was listening to the second and third and fourth graders. Really, that's the way we learned.

At Rocky Top Camp we did the same thing at school, but at recess, since we were parked right at the foot of a butte, we would climb up the butte for exercise and just for fun. In the wintertime we would take our sleds up and slide down right across the tracks right past the schoolhouse and halfway down into camp. It was great! They had a path cleared that froze after a while so it was pretty fast, like ice.

I took my lunch in a five-pound lard pail. That's the way we got our lard. We had butter or we had lard. The pail had a handle and a lid. My dad liked baking powder biscuits for breakfast, so for lunch we had baking powder biscuits with peanut butter and jelly and usually some fruit of some kind. In the schoolhouse there was a bucket with water in it and a long-handled dipper. When we were thirsty we took turns and all drank out of that dipper. It's a wonder we weren't all dead from it, but as far as I can remember we didn't have any outbreaks of illnesses.

The schoolhouses were used for social halls too. If they wanted to have a square dance or movies, they'd push the desks back against the walls. There were also box socials. The women would all prepare a fancy box of some kind. My mother used a rolled oats box one time. They'd fry chicken and make sandwiches and bake cake or pie and pack it in the boxes. Then they'd take 'em to the social and the men would bid on them. The one who bid the highest on each particular box ate supper with the lady who brought the box. No one knew who made each box. They didn't know what was in the box either. They just bid on the appearance of the box. The women would decorate them with crepe paper or cutouts and things like that. If the box was big and very pretty, why sometimes they'd bid quite a bit.

I'll tell you about the teacher. She not only had to teach that many children and that many grades, but she had to carry in the wood, make the fire in the stove, and do the dusting and the sweeping too, so she was really both the janitor and the teacher. The rule in Bend was that teachers had to be single. During the school year she either lived in a house or she lived with a family. The families were good to the teachers and invited them to meals and things, but since they didn't like to be with the bunkhouse men and there were no other young people in the camps, they were lonely. So lonely, that they never stayed more than a year.

I loved school and looked forward to it. During the summer, I could barely wait for it to start again. While school was out, we took off our shoes and ran barefooted all summer long. Then in September we had to go to town and buy new shoes. With our new shoes on and our lunch pails in hand, we headed back to our boxcar schoolhouse and another year of learning adventures.

Alice (Nelson) Bishop is a native of Bend, born in 1914. As early homesteaders, her family came to the Northwest in a covered wagon. Her father worked for Brooks-Scanlon and she attended school in the logging camps. She married her husband Leo in 1935 and raised three sons.

Lemon Sauce

Bring to boil:
1/2 cup sugar
1 T. cornstarch
1 cup water

Cook until thick and clear about 5 minutes.
Add:
1 t. butter
1 1/2 T. lemon juice
dash of nutmeg and salt

Serve with steaming pudding.

Taken from **Holiday Potpourri** *by Vi Shepard*

From Knot Bumper to President
Mel McClain

My folks moved to Bend in 1918 when I was two years old. I started school in 1922 at Young School out on Butler Market Road near where the Bend Airport is now. It was only a one-room school the first four years I went there. Then they built a new one - two rooms and a basement. And that's where the first school hot lunch program in Bend started. Kids would bring food from home to make something for lunch and one of the mother's or somebody else would be assigned to go down to the basement and make the soup, or whatever it was we were having. So, we'd have a hot lunch. 'Course, you didn't have a choice of what you wanted to eat.

In 1930, I started high school. I went out for football and in spring training I broke my leg. I just lay there on the sideline for an hour until they got through practice before they took me to see the doctor. He put a cast on my leg and told my dad to bring me back the next day. My dad did and the doctor cut that cast off. Then they took an x-ray and told me my leg was crooked. So they straightened her out and put another cast on. I don't remember they gave me anything to ease the pain. It cost my dad $25 to get my leg fixed and he said, "I don't think we can afford that anymore."

In gym class one day, I was sitting on this bar and I kicked my feet over the top of my head and fell backwards and landed on the mat. I put my right arm back to catch myself and broke my wrist. I forget who the gym instructor was, but he told some other kid to go with me down to Dr. Vandevert's office. Doc Vandevert took hold of my arm and my wrist and went like that and popped it back in place. Then he put a metal deal on my arm and said, "Go back to school."

I graduated in 1934 but couldn't get a job so I joined the Civilian Conservation Corps. They were looking for young guys. Shevlin-Hixon and the Forest Service had a big land exchange going on, exchanging land for trees. We'd go out in three men crews and tally the trees. We also rated the land as being A Land, B Land, C Land, or D Land, depending on how many trees were growing there. They based the value of the land on what we were doing.

Whether we did it right or not, I don't know. We spent most of our time at Spring River in what was called a 'spike' camp.

The main camp was at Odell Lake and I went up there until they closed that camp. Then they took us over to Fall Creek just outside of Eugene and I worked there for a year until the following December. I learned to drive a truck and a Cat bulldozer and I learned how to build roads. My salary was $30 a month. I put $5 dollars in my pocket and sent $25 home to my mother who saved it for me.

My dad was working the logging woods, so when I got out in December of '35 I went to work with him. We worked on Brooks-Scanlon land for a contractor by the name of Bill Crawford. A year or so later I went to work for a fellow by the name of Anthony Roach. That was in Sisters out at Petersen's Mill. I was just a knot bumper in those days. For two years I worked bumping knots and driving horses, things like that. Then in 1938 they let me start driving the truck to haul the logs. Anthony Roach owned the truck, but I was driving it.

Shevlin - Hixon

In those days there weren't any safety programs for logging. Period. There wasn't anything to hold the logs on the truck while you were carrying them. We just put what we called cheese blocks on the bottom and a sink-chain around the middle of the load. You'd load some logs on and then put the sink-chain on to squeeze the logs down. Then you'd bring them in. You had to dump the load by hand. I've had to get under my truck and knock the chain loose so the logs would fall off on both sides of the truck while I was under the truck. Despite that, we didn't have too many accidents that I can remember.

When I was drafted in November of 1941 I was 25 years old and single. I wanted to get into flying, but even though I had a private pilot's license I couldn't because at that time you needed to have two years of college. After Pearl Harbor they changed the requirements and I finally got to fly. I flew a B-17, then a B-24, and ended up flying lead pilot on a B-24. In all I flew 52 missions before it was over and I was wounded on the last one.

Before the war, I had worked with a fellow named Harold Barclay. While I was gone he was able to get a logging company of his own. He'd been over to see me a couple of times while I was still in the service, and he asked me to work with him. I got out because I had a wife and we had two children at the time. I brought my family back home to Bend and I went to work for Harold in Sisters. We logged in the Sisters area, in the Warm Springs Indian Reservation, in the Mt. Hood National Forest, and south and east of Bend. I worked for Harold from '46 until I retired in '82 or '83 and went from knot bumper to president of that company.

Except my time in the service, I spent my life in the logging business. I rated and tallied trees, bumped knots, hauled logs and managed men in the forest. Before my working days were over, I served on the Board of Directors for the Oregon Logging Conference and was even elected president one year. It was a long way from knot bumper to president of the company and along the way I guess I about did it all.

Mel McClain, b.1916 in Michigan, moved to Central Oregon as a young boy in 1918. He served in the Air Force earning a Silver Star and the Distinguished Flying Cross. He worked in the logging industry for many years.

Clark Gable's Days in Bend

George McGeary, M.D.

In 1957 there were still quite a few loggers and mill workers in Bend who claimed they knew and worked with the man who called himself "Billy Gable" in 1922, but today these co-workers are long gone from the scene.

In the early days in Hollywood, the rumors were that Clark Gable's real name was William Clark Gable, but his birth records, baptismal records and school records list him only as Clark or Clarke Gable. He was born February 1, 1901 in Cadiz, Ohio, and his mother died a year later. His father, Will Gable, was a handsome oilfield "wildcatter" who was constantly on the move. He turned young Clark over to relatives to raise and that had a profound effect on his son. Despite his later successes there was a withdrawing and a void that Clark was seeking to fill and he was always called "shy."

By the time Will quit wildcatting for oil and bought a farm where he and his son could live, Clark was big, strong, athletic and ready to take off himself. He dropped out of high school, left home, worked at various jobs for awhile, and renamed himself "Billy" because the laborers he worked with thought "Clark" was a sissy name. He worked at hard manual labor but always had an eye for the theatre and acting.

Perpetually short of money, he had a legacy of $300 waiting for him when he turned twenty-one. When that day arrived he promptly collected the money. Then he joined a travelling tent show and was paid $10 a week for hawking playbills and performing at night. Clark felt he was more appreciated for his brawn in taking the tent down and putting it up than for his acting ability. The troupe collapsed in Butte, Montana. Clark was too broke to leave town. Phil, the pianist in the tent show, said he had an uncle in Bend, Oregon who could finance them so the two headed west. When they arrived in Bend in 1922, the uncle could not be found and Clark was forced to work as a lumberjack and in a sawmill.

His fellow workmen who were still here in 1957 described Clark as a "stage-struck" youngster who just "mooned around." Clark's description taken from a 1940 <u>Saturday Evening Post</u> article differed considerably. In it he said:

"I got a job piling green logs. All the fellows worked by the foot. They worked hard. They made me work hard too. Probably the toughest work I ever did. The logs were rough, of course, and heavy, and I had no gloves. They all wore leather gloves or a leather palm. I'd tie into that lumber and it was like grabbing hold of sandpaper. I used to soak my hands; they had cuts in them and would be stiff and crack open. I'd soak them in salt water and vinegar to toughen them. Alum, too. I had hands like a prize fighter until I got my first paycheck and got my gloves, but I didn't use them until I got my hands all hardened up and toughened."

Clark was sick, tired, and miserable, but he piled logs until late in the spring, when he finally had enough money to get to Portland. Friends in Portland described him as having a yellow cast to his skin at that time. His illness in Bend could have been jaundice from hepatitis.

He got a temporary job at Meier and Frank's Department Store in Portland, and to his good fortune, the man selling at the counter next to him was Earle Larimore, a handsome, aristocratic young man, whose family had been prominent in the theatrical world.

Earle was acting and directing in a local Portland group called the Red Lantern Players. Clark Gable joined up. From there he went on to the Astoria Players Stock Company and fell in love with a fellow actress, but married instead a much older woman named Josephine Dillon. A well-known drama coach, she was just the first of his five wives, albeit a very important one for the role she played in shaping his future. With the rough edges knocked off and a lot of polishing, Clark Gable was on his way to three decades of super stardom.

As for Bend, in truth I cannot tell you how well he was really known to the loggers I talked to in 1957. But Clark Gable did remember the few months he worked in Bend, and usually referred to this part of his life in the many interviews he gave during his career.

George McGeary, M.D. was a pathologist in Bend for many years. He writes and has an interest in local history.

From Walton's Mountain to Bend - A Place Called Home
Norma Gene (Moore) Rennolds

In 1922 the recommended mode of traveling long distance was by rail. The Model T Ford was fine in the city limits, but for the long journey, the trains were more reliable.

It was on a cold November day that Mother boarded the train with her three children. She was leaving Tekoa, Washington with Virginia - age 4, Merle - age 2, and Norma Gene - 10 months. She said her good-byes to her parents and, with tears and excitement, she headed south to that little mill town of Bend that H. A. Miller of the Miller Lumber Company had written so glowingly about.

Mother, Josephine Moore, came to join her husband, Frank, who had preceded her to Bend a few weeks earlier to find a house to live in and reassure her that Bend was indeed a thriving lumber and timber community. Dad had been employed by Potlatch Lumber Company in Tekoa as a bookkeeper, so he was knowledgeable in that field. Mother loved Bend at first sight.

Dad went to work for Mr. Miller at the office on Wall Street and continued in his employ for many years. After the Depression, he changed occupations to the hardware business. He owned and operated Midstate Hardware next door to Wetles Department Store on Wall Street until he decided to "go wholesale" and put in a warehouse near the railroad just off the Franklin Avenue underpass. Until his death at age seventy-four, he and Mother were equal partners in the business, Oregon Hardware Distributing.

We lived on Broadway Street and I remember it before it was paved. A tree grew right in the middle of it and people drove around it. Mother lived in that little house on Broadway for over seventy years, long after we girls were married and gone our separate ways.

As a little child, I would sit on our parking strip and wait for Mr. Ray. He drove the wood wagon and delivered boxwood to the mill families for their cook stoves. The wood was scraps from the box factory at the mill where the workers made apple boxes and orange crates. Mr. Ray would let me go on his rounds to deliver the wood. In today's day and age, no mother would let her little girl do such a thing as ride with an older man, but in 1927, we knew almost every-one in town and Mom knew he was an honorable man.

We girls attended Reid school through the first three grades. I had Miss Jean Webster in the second grade. She was my favorite teacher of all time. I remember how she placed little wooden chairs in a semi-circle. We students sat in them and faced her while she taught us phonics, the method to teach us beginners to read and enunciate. Her teaching helped me more than any other teacher in the pronunciation and spelling of words.

While I never attended any of her "latter day" tea parties, she came to one that Mother had for her. I was so pleased to think she would come to our house. Just Mother and Miss Webster and a pleased seven-year-old, she made me feel special.

After school, we changed clothes from dresses to bib overalls, not because they were "trendy," but because they wore like iron and cost $2.98. Who could possibly look down the years to come and foresee that denim jeans would cost big bucks and make a desir-able fashion statement?

When I look back on those years of my life in Bend, it reminds me of TV's "The Waltons." We all had chores to do and we bickered over whose turn it was to do what. Mine was always keeping the wood box filled for the kitchen range. Mother baked filled cookies to be sold to Erickson's Market for resale to the mill workers for lunch. I made lots of trips to the woodpile to keep the cook stove hot. Mother would say, "Norma Gene, if you let my fire go out, I'll get a switch from the willow tree." That always got my attention.

Mother also baked angel food cakes for the weddings in our little Christian church. She would tell us not to slam the door or the cake would fall. We really didn't mean to jar the oven, but I can still savor how wonderful those fallen cakes tasted.

We lived in an era of unlocked doors. There were lots of hobos during the Depression. Mother fed all that knocked on her door, but never until they earned it by stacking a little wood or hoeing a row of the garden. She said if they worked a little, it would "save their dignity." We didn't realize until years later that they had marked the telephone poles to let other hobos know that our house was a sure meal.

Bend was like Walton's Mountain; everyone knew everyone. No use trying to fool anybody; everyone knew you and your folks.

Very few high school students had cars. When we asked our folks how we could get to the game or the dance, the standard answer was, "On shank's mare," which meant - walk!!

And walk we did. I think that is why my generation is still around to talk about the old days. We walked because it was necessary.

I think Bend started changing when the mills lost their status as the backbone of our local economy. The metamorphosis was slow, but sure. The transformation is now complete from mill town to city, from larva to butterfly. It seems that now most people come here, not to work, but to retire, to ski, to fish, to hunt, to enjoy the arts.

Bend isn't a Walton's Mountain kind of place anymore. Too much has changed for that. The only thing that hasn't changed, and never will, is the beauty of this place called Bend. The mountain views, the lakes and the grandeur of this high desert country, Central Oregon - a place called home.

Norma (Moore) Rennolds has lived in Central Oregon since November 1922, nearly all her life. She worked in her husband Lee's accounting business and is a proud member of PEO. Lee Rennolds' family donated the land for the Central Oregon District Hospital.

A Pound of This, and a Pound of That

Rolie Anderson

From a panel discussion moderated by Paul Reynolds on April 25, 2000

My mother traded at Erickson's, came home from the store one day and said Mr. Erickson's looking for a young boy to work for him. I got the job and worked there from 1929 to 1935.

The retail clerks were working to form a union. Erickson's was the only grocery being picketed. I was assistant manager at the time and didn't have to join the union. But my friends at Erickson's were walking the picket line. I couldn't cross that line, seeing my friends there. So I quit and walked across the street to Piggly Wiggly and was hired on the spot for the assistant manager and produce manager job. I worked there for 26 years until the owner, Mr. Meyers, died. From there I went to Wagners for two years and then I bought the Piggly Wiggly store myself. I had it 10 years and made a nice living out of it.

Back then we did a lot of our business by telephone. Customers called their orders in and we delivered. We had one customer who really had to work to make her money go as far as it needed to, and every payday she would call and order a pound of everything on her list. That's because everything was in bulk. Flour come in 50-pound sacks and 25-pound bags. We used to weigh up our own sugar, put it in 10-pound bags, double the bags, wrap 'em, and put string around 'em. Everything that was bought, we'd put it up as we sold it, and we didn't have the packaging supplies we have today like plastic bags and cellophane tape.

I did a little research on some prices. This come out of a 1932 ad in Bend. Potatoes, 20 lbs. for 49 cents. A 2-lb. jar of peanut butter, 23 cents. Bacon, 15 cents a lb., sugar 10 lb. for 47 cents and Sanka coffee, 29 cents a pound. The S & M Men's Shop across the street was selling shirts for 65 cents each. Toilet paper was 5 cents a roll, and that brings up a story.

Kate Rockwell traded at Erickson's. One day she came in and ordered 3 rolls of toilet paper and a broom. I got them for her and asked, "Mrs. Rockwell, can I put that in a sack for you?" She said,

"Nah," and put the toilet paper on the broom handle, put the broom handle over her shoulder and strolled out of the store.

In some ways the grocery business has changed a lot. It used to be that you would get to know people real well. If they'd come in and be short of money, you'd loan it to them, or let 'em charge their groceries, that type of thing.

The only thing is, I got $65 a month. That was for all the hours they wanted to work us. We worked from 8:00 a.m. 'till 6:00 p.m., or as long as they wanted to keep us. They closed on Sundays and holidays, but on holidays they always brought us back to do some work, changing the store. One time we wanted a raise in salary, we figured we was getting 10 cents an hour.

But we had fun too. I'll never forget, the Pilot Butte Inn was owned by Harry Brooks. He come from England. He brought a Plymouth Touring car here. The top went down and in the wintertime you put the top up. It was right-hand drive. A friend of mine, Waymon Mauer, bought that. So, we'd cruise. Waymon, he'd scoot way down in the right-hand side and the rest of us would scoot way down on the other side. It didn't look like there was anyone driving. So, we got the idea one Sunday, we went and got a steering post and steering wheel, the whole assembly, and took off to Redmond. Waymon was driving. He was down low so no one could see him. So, Burl, my friend would stand up on the left-hand side, turn around, face backwards with the steering wheel up in the air. People were driving off the road. "There's a maniac out there, there's a maniac out there." We had more fun with that. Pretty soon they turned us in, a State Policeman come and stopped us. He didn't give us a ticket or anything but he just laughed and said we better stop that. But we sure had a lot of fun with that right-hand drive Plymouth!

Roland Anderson, b. 1915 in North Dakota, moved to Bend in 1929. He married the "prettiest little gal in town", Francis Jordan. After retiring from the grocery business he has been very active with the Deschutes County Historical Society.

Dr. Grant Skinner, Bend's Single Parent Dentist

Barbara Buxton

My father, Dr. Grant Skinner, migrated from North Dakota to the Hermiston area when he was four years old. His father dreamed of one of his sons becoming a farmer, but the older sons had no interest in plowing the earth. Dad was given a field to farm and he did give it a try. During the day he would do field work, but evenings he helped a local dentist in his lab. One day, while plowing the field, the harness broke and Dad fell on his face in the dirt. That was the end of his farming days. He got up, went to his father and announced that he was going to Portland to become a dentist.

To pay his way through college, he worked nights, stoking the furnace in the building where he lived. During World War I, he and the other students were drafted into the Army. They were issued uniforms, bunked together in a dormitory and allowed to continue their education. Luckily, they were never called up to serve. He graduated in 1919, after the Armistice was signed. At 23, he was the youngest graduate up to that date.

His older bother, who had the general store in Tumalo, encouraged him to come to Bend. Dad took the train to Deschutes Junction, and walked from there to Tumalo. The following day my uncle brought him in to Bend where he found a room to rent. He set up practice in the O'Kane Building across the hall from Dr. Wyn Manning, the only other dentist in town who had arrived shortly before.

Eventually, Dad rented an office on the second floor of a building on Wall. He hired a painter to put his name on the window. When it was completed, he stood out in the middle of the street gazing up at the window, admiring how good it looked. A man approached him, puzzled at what he was looking at. Pointing to the window, dad replied gleefully, "That's me!" That was his introduction to the man who was to become his best friend, Jep Smith.

A few years later Dad influenced his cousins, Drs. Robert and Max Hemingway, to move to Bend and set up their medical practice. They built the building at 1036 Wall Street where the two of them and dad practiced for many years. After Dr. Bob's death, his brother renamed their practice the Robert Hemingway Memorial Clinic. Later it became the Bend Memorial Clinic.

Dad married my mother, Margaret, in 1923. I was just a year old when Mother died in 1931, and Father raised my sister and me by himself. That was really unheard of in those days, but he was a good single parent, and I remember those years as the happiest of my life. He didn't have to do the cleaning as we had a live-in housekeeper who worked for room and board and very little pay.

With the lumber mills being the sole support of the town, business was good, but the ability to pay during the Depression was far from ideal. I remember my sister and I going out to patients' homes during that time to try to collect what we could. We got 50 cents here and 50 cents there, but in those days 50 cents was a lot of money. Farmers in the area paid in chickens, eggs, pork, and what they had on hand.

One of the stories my dad liked to tell was about my mother's bootlegging brother who would come through Bend during the Prohibition years. Mother was adamantly against drinking. She didn't have a clue her brother was transporting liquor up and down the Willamette Valley by coming over to Highway 97 to avoid the Feds, and both of them made sure she never found out. When he was in town, he and Dad would slip out to my uncle's car to have a quick drink, and there in the false bottom of the trunk were gallon jugs of bootleg booze.

There were good stories about Dad too. Winters were cold and insulation rare in the 1930's, so Dad wrapped the pipes under the house in old tire inner tubes. One morning he went down to thaw the pipes and set the rubber on fire. The firemen came and put it out, and then Chief Tom Carlon gave my sister and me a lecture on the dangers of playing with matches! We kept our mouths shut and took the rap for Dad that time.

There was also the time Dad hit the train. At the time there was no Franklin Street underpass and one dark, rainy night he was stopped at the railroad tracks. Dad couldn't see the train in front of him so when the railroad worker started swinging his lantern, he thought he meant for him to proceed. He did, and ran right into the train.

I can also remember a time when Dad was called out to a small farm on the east side of town to pull a dog's infected tooth. What a story that pooch must have had to tell his four-legged pals.

Times were lean in those years before WW II, but when Camp Abbot came to the area, and Dad was awarded the Army Dental Contract, things began to look up for him financially. He cleaned, filled, pulled and replaced teeth here from 1919 to 1973, and it's not unusual to run into an old-timer who still remembers his days in Dad's dental chair.

Barbara (Skinner) Buxton, b. 1929 in Bend is the daughter of Dr. Grant Skinner. She attended Kenwood Elementary and Bend High School. She still lives in Bend.

Grant Skinner, 1919
Graduation from Pacific Dental College

Would You Call That a Proposal?
Emmlie Starr

Around 1934 I moved to Powell Butte. I was 24 years old and working at McDaniel's General Store which was the only one out there at that time. It was right across the road from the Powell Butte School and it sold everything from soup to nuts and steaks. And then it had the post office. There was also another little building on the side that was a hardware store. We kept the key and when somebody needed some hardware, one of us would run over and get it.

You want to know how I met my husband, Vern? Gosh, one day I looked out that store door, and saw a tall, dark and handsome guy out at the gas pump. He had blue eyes but black hair. Oh, he was handsome. I asked Grandma McDaniel, "Who's the good lookin' guy out there?" She said, "Oh, he's just back from herding sheep. He's herding sheep and goin' to college in the wintertime." And she said, "His folks live out here and he's the nicest guy. They call him "Rev." I told her that if he was a minister he wouldn't want to have nothin' to do with me. "Well anyhow," she said "that's just a nickname because he's such a nice fellar."

He come to the door and wanted some hardware, so I said to Grandma Mac, "Give me that key quick and I'll take care of him." He wanted a lock washer. I looked at him and I didn't say anything. They say if you're dumb, you make it. Boy, growin' up with seven brothers I knew all about hardware, but I pretended not to know what I was lookin' for. I was the dumbest thing you ever heard of for a clerk. Later on he found out and he'd like 'ta shot me.

Anyhow, he started to look for it himself. Finally he found the lock washer and he took one out. He was the kind of person who would hold something out and he had to tell you every little bit about it. That's the way he was; he should have been an instructor. And so, he went on and he's explaining how it worked. It was awful hard for me to keep from laughing. I knew as much or more as he did about the darn lock washer.

Anyhow, he says, "Are you going to go to the harvest ball?" It was coming up on that weekend. I said, "Oh I don't know, if the road isn't crowded." I never played a game like that in my life before, never had a reason to. So he says, "Well I'll be by and get you about 7:30." That was a date. That's the way he handled it. He came by and took me to the dance, and he was a beautiful dancer. I knew then I just had to hang in there.

Two days later Vern came by on a Sunday and he said, "Would you like to go for a drive?" I told him, "Well I'm just going out to my folks." Momma always had a big deal on Sundays, so we went out there. I had explained to him that I had lost a husband to cancer of the lung and had a little girl of four named Patty. She was a cute little bug with curls and all.

That day Patty watched him for a long time. Finally she came over beside his chair and looked at him. He picked her up on his lap and she said, "Will you be my daddy?" That poor guy. One of my brothers, he had to go outside to laugh and he says to me, "Em, you sure got that kid trained." And Vern, he says, "Well, we'll have to see what your mother has to say about that." Then he never said a word to me anymore than hello, goodbye and he just took me back to work.

He came by after work about four or five days later and he said, "I've got something I want to show ya'." That was the third time I'd seen him. So, I got in the car and he took me down and showed me the homestead. "Now that's mine," he told me "and it can be yours too, if you want it." I looked at it - all that sagebrush and rock, and I didn't say anything because I didn't know what to say.

A few days later he came in and said, "I got George Cox to go with me and we went to Prineville and got the marriage license." He never asked, "Will you marry me?" or anything. He talked to my kid, but he never asked me. He just did it. I never said yes or no. I was just stunned.

Towards the end of the week he came in and he says, "Well I set up everything with the minister." He had about eight people there at the minister's house across from the store. It was a Presbyterian Church and I was raised a Catholic, but I wasn't going to argue over it. Old Grandma Mac kept telling me, "He's a wonderful catch, he's a wonderful catch." I was preached that every day. And then that kid was hangin' on saying, "Momma I want him for a daddy."

And that's the way the whole thing happened. Six weeks after we met, we got married, and we had been married for sixty-two years when he passed away. It worked out pretty well, you know.

Emmlie (Urell) Starr was born in 1909 in the Dakota Territory. She moved to the Powell Butte area in the early 1930s. Vern Starr was born in 1907 above Prineville. She was a teacher, bookkeeper, clerk, cow herder and horseback rider. She currently lives in Redmond and still makes dolls and paints.

To me, fair friend, you never can be old,
For as you were when first your eye I eyed,
Such seems your beauty still.

From Sonnet 104
By William Shakespeare (1564-1616)

A Hard, Wild, Buckarooing Life

Martha Stranahan, excerpted from the Central Electric <u>Ruralite</u>, 1964

"If I had it all to do over again what would I do different? Be just a little bit wilder—ride more wild horses.

I buckarooed all my life," reminisced Earl Fowler, meditatively drawing on a cigarette, his dark, slicked-back hair and bright eyes belying his professed age. "Never see 70 again."

He'd be buckarooing still, probably, had not the last bone breakage, in 1955, been a double jolt that shelved him for six months. One time a nurse, contemplating his X-rays, inquired if he had a whole bone in his body.

Fowler was born "just 52 miles north of Dodge City." During Kansas blizzards ranchers found their way from house to barn by means of a guide rope tied between the two. He grew up ranching and riding, and at age 15 walked—not ran—away from home. In Colorado he hired out as a wrangler and night herder.

There were no corrals or fences in those days, so the buckaroos worked shifts at night herding the horses and cattle. Once he was called to relieve the "nighthawk" who took sick. It was drizzling rain and the horses stampeded. Earl figured they had probably smelled bear. They like to travel in rain, he added.

The herders on the ponies ran the scattering horses most of the night. They jumped ditches which they, and probably their mounts, wouldn't assay in daytime—washes 20 feet deep and as far across. But the horses had the "feel of the ground." They would rear and snort, and riders would brace for another jump. By daylight the superintendent met them — 14 miles from camp. What breed of horses were they? Just horses, says Fowler, adding there was more Morgan in them than is common now.

He buckarooed in Texas and New Mexico, rode in cow stampedes, herded horses and cattle. For recreation the cowboys would hold "celebrations" (forerunner of today's rodeos), one ranch against the other.

In the spring of 1938 he came to the old ZX ranch in Paisley, and remained with the outfit 17 years. His cabin was at Brown's Valley, between Hampton and Brothers, and there he kept a string of horses, always including one of his own. He would ride the circle all day, trailing cattle, and each morning saddle up a fresh pony.

What varied the routine of riding, roping, trailing for a desert buckaroo? One time, riding in Sheep Rock country, he killed 32 rattlers in a day. Once he came upon a coyote pup and used it to work a horse he was training. That coyote was tuckered out, but the horse got the idea and switched easily to a calf, Fowler says. Riding one day in 1942 he came to a homesteader's one-room cabin, the door padlocked. Through the dusty window he saw an old cookstove with rusted pipe, a broken chair, a bed made up but crumbly with dust and age—and a wall calendar dated June, 1911! Another defeated homesteader had just walked away from it all.

And then on a day in 1955, he was shoeing a horse (spoiled critter, he recalls, wryly), in his cabin corral when the horse kicked him, snapped the hitch, sailed over the fence and away. Fowler's right leg was broken square across below the knee and above the ankle. Propping his broken leg on his good one he managed to drag himself into his cabin, but not before a tapioca snow had soaked him.

He could shut the door but not the windows, and could light no fire; and he cussed that horse. Two days later Ellis Painter, running horses in the area, dropped by "to see how you're getting along."

"A man with a broken leg ain't doing very well," Earl told him.

Painter rode 20 miles, returned with his pickup, an old pair of crutches, a large grocery carton padded with blankets, and some pain pills. He bound Fowler's leg lightly to the padded box and they were ready to take off — only the pickup wouldn't start. But it had a crank, too, and that worked. Fowler dozed, awoke outside Central Oregon District Hospital in Redmond, and spent six months there recovering from double troubles — pneumonia and a broken leg.

Fowler returned for a part of a year with ZX—close to headquarters—then retired to Redmond. On Thursdays at Redmond Auction Yard he rides and heads the buyer's cattle into pens after they leave the sales ring. He rides as deputy at rodeos, or he visits with cronies downtown and talks of buckaroo days. At home he raises a few chicken, pastures Buck, the 19-year-old buckskin pony he rode many years with ZX—and wishes he had ridden wilder and harder.

Jess Eddington

Cold Nights, Hot Beans, and One Wrong Turn On the Way to Elk Lake

Georgia Edgington Gallagher

During the summer of '38 my brother, Jess Edgington, had a concession for furnishing saddle horses and packhorses at the Elk Lake pack station. He was running it for a man who had concessions all up and down the Cascades, called Mac Hugh Tours. Jess did this during the summer to earn money for college. It was his responsibility to get the horses to the Elk Lake pack station.

The distance from the Edgington Ranch two miles south of Sisters to Elk Lake, by way of Three Creeks and the mountain road over Broken Top to Todd Lake, is approximately thirty miles. About 10:00 a.m. on June 7th, Jess and I and two of his friends, Chuck and Paul Christy started from the ranch with nine horses. The road was clear of snow for about fifteen miles into Three Creeks Meadow.

76

We rode four of the horses, leading the other five, including an old Appaloosa packhorse named Fiddle. I can remember Jess tying one horse's tail to another's lead rope. It saved one person at a time from leading two horses. Fiddle carried our camping equipment. My father would be taking the rest of Jess' equipment and supplies by way of Bend and then Century Drive.

As I remember, there was a bit of fresh snow on the road that would cake on the horses' hooves. We spent the first night at Three Creeks Meadow. At the time there was a Forest Service cabin there on a little knoll, and we were able to get in, though I can't remember if it was locked or not. We may have climbed in the window. There was a wood stove to build a fire and keep us warm. The horses were hobbled in the early evening so they could graze, but we tied them up at night so they wouldn't go back home.

When evening fell on the second night we camped along a beautiful little mountain stream, and cooked both supper and breakfast over a campfire. It was pretty cold and we all bundled up close together to keep warm.

The road over the mountains to Todd Lake goes east from the Three Creeks Meadow area, around the end of McArthur Rim, and over to the headwaters of Tumalo Creek. There's a junction where the road over the mountain and the road into Tumalo Creek join. When we reached that junction we took the wrong turn and headed left instead of right. We traveled three or four miles before we realized what we had done, turned around and started back up the trail the way we had come. By the time we reached Happy Valley in the headwaters of Tumalo Creek, it was late so we decided to camp there for the night. We had expected to be all the way over the mountains by that evening, but the extra eight miles we had to travel when we took the wrong turn made it too late to continue that night.

When morning came we started across a higher section of the narrow road. There was still a heavy snow pack on the ground, it was hilly, and the horses slipped and skidded on the icy surface. Because the clouds hung low and you couldn't see the mountains, we weren't sure we were going in the right direction and that was cause for real concern. Though the snow was still pretty heavy, it was melting underneath in the creek channels and the old long-legged Appaloosa, Fiddle caved through the snow into the creek a couple of times. She tried to get out by herself, but couldn't with the heavy pack, so we had to take it off to get her up.

We finally came to a well-used trail with recent boot tracks and followed them to a cabin. It was used by people working on the Crater Ditch that diverted water into the Tumalo drainage from Broken Top crater. We found one of the workers in that nice warm cabin and he had a big pot of beans on the stove, which he offered us for lunch. I don't think that there were many beans left after the four of us finished.

It was about 3:00 in the afternoon, and there was lots of daylight left in the long spring day. He told us to follow his tracks out to the road that went down to Todd Lake, which we did. As we came out we were met by state policemen who were contemplating sending out a search party for us, because we were supposed to be there the day before. My parents had been there waiting for us, and when we didn't come they went back home and reported us missing.

As I recall, the police gave me a ride home and my brother and his two friends proceeded on to Elk Lake with the horses. I remember being anxious to get home, not because I recognized the danger we had been in when we got lost in the mountains, but because I had a big date for that night. After all, I was sixteen.

Georgia (Edgington) Gallagher, born in Sisters, Oregon. She was raised and is presently living on the Edgington ranch just south of Sisters. She worked as a dietician in State of Oregon institutions.

Georgia Eddington

Forest Fires, Cougars, and Bristly Short Hairs

Kenneth "Mac" McKenzie

In the summer of 1933 I was home from Monmouth College and working for the Forest Service. Leo Houston and I were put at Box Canyon. Now this was an unusual thing, because they never did use two Forest Guards at one station - but they did there! We would take turns walking to Taylor Burn (west of Cultus Lake) and back - so we had a 15-mile round trip. Every day one of us would walk that beautiful trail and enjoy the birds and chipmunks, and the other one would cook.

Things went along well, and we didn't have any fires for quite awhile. Then one day she clouded up and just let us have it! The big shot was up on Grasshopper Mountain, about 10 miles from Box Canyon. The only way to get to it was to go up over Chuseney, down in a canyon, and back up on Grasshopper. So we both went, 'cause they really had a bunch of fires started up there! When we got there, it was so bad we found out that we just plain couldn't handle it ourselves.

It became a question of which one of us would go back to the telephone, 'cause in those days everything was telephone if you had any connection at all. Well, I drew the short straw. It was getting late and it was a hard trail, an old Indian one that went down into a canyon, back up on top, and then down again. So I took off . . . no light . . . nothing. . . but I figured I could make it if I really picked 'em up and laid 'em down!

Going down into the canyon that I had to climb out of, everything was rosy until I got down into the bottom and I discovered there was a nice fat cougar lookin' at me. But he was quite a little ways off, and he didn't look dangerous or anything like that. However, I've been in the mountains all of my life, and I am still afraid of a cougar if he's got just himself and I got just myself. If I got a gun, well that's diff'rent, but I didn't have one, and I had a long way to go and I figured, well, there's just one thing to do. You just walk, and walk at the same gait, but that's very hard to do. It was tempting to run, but you never run, just never run. That would be the worst thing you could do - cause he'd have you! I didn't have a rifle, didn't have a gun of any sort, the only thing I had was a nice

79

pole I found. And I thought if he tried to go and get ahead of me and to attack me from a limb, I'd have a slight chance.

Well, I kept a goin' and I was a climbin' up the trail and ever once in a while I'd see him, but just a flash of 'em. Of course, that didn't help my blood pressure any. I kept goin' at the same speed and ever'thing, and if he was going' to eat me, well, he'd just have to eat me!

I'd gotten into lots of discussions in college over whether a person's hair would stand out on the short part around the ears and so on, if he got scared bad enough. Well, this is a test I took! I was scared. I wore an old red hunting cap that I pertneer always wore that time of the year, and I could pull that hat down as hard as I could on my head. Now I had the presence of mind to do this, 'cuz if I was gonna live, I would have proof that it would either loosen that hat up, or it wouldn't.

So I walked, and I walked, and I tried my best to keep an even stride, and I think I did very well. I still had prob'ly nearly 5 miles to go and it was gettin' darker and darker and ever once in a while I'd see that stinker out to the side aways, so I knew he wasn't givin' up. Well, I walked at a regular pace but I think I took longer steps because I didn't want to let him know that I was scared, and I was scared. I got very close to Box Canyon and I thought, boy if I can make it another hunnerd yards I'd have it and I did. I made it the next hunnerd yards or I wouldn't be tellin' this!

Well now for this hat business . . . I didn't just do that once. I did it quite a number of times to be sure I was right. I'd pull my cap down as tight as I could get it on my head and I'd walk 50 yards or less and I could reach up with my hand and knock it off my head. I am not saying the hair on the top, the long hair. I'm quite sure that it doesn't stand up, but this short hair, the bristly stuff around the edge definitely will do it and I'm proof of it. There's no question in my mind that hair bristles - but what a way to win an argument!

Mac McKenzie, b. 1909 in Scott's Mill, Oregon.
He taught school and served in the Marine Corps
in WWII. He and his wife owned a sporting good
store in Crescent, Oregon, where he was
instrumental in starting Midstate Electric.
He now lives in Bend.

The Bend Water Pageant

Almost from its beginning, the little frontier village of Bend made traditional and patriotic observance of the nation's birthday. Fourth of July entertainment grew with the town, somehow into two and even three-day celebrations with programming that reflected the little community's interests and history.

Then in June 1933, in the midst of the Depression, someone on the planning committee had a new idea: why not use the Deschutes River in the setting of Drake Park for water sports of various kinds? Why not a night pageant with floats and lights, and music, people and . .! The idea fired the imagination, almost eclipsing other traditional events.

The committee worked out a three day schedule (July 2,3,4) crammed with events. There would be baseball, fireworks, rodeo, prize fights, a street parade, a pet parade, music, dancing, a Queen's contest and a "river fete."

1933's celebration was a rousing success and the very best part was the river event. Pacific Power & Light crews erected wooden towers along the edges of the park and mounted large, movable floodlights. There were 19 floats. The little flotilla, some carrying passengers, was led by the Queen's barge pulled by a giant wooden swan, image of the proud and stately resident swans of the park.

A surprise feature was the appearance of a night flier whose plane dipped over the park and river with red flares on the wings. Ted Barber was the pilot. Ben Whisenand had charge of the fireworks display which became a traditional part of the river show.This first venture set the pattern; in 1934 the energies focused on bigger and better, and there was a new title, "The Bend Water Pageant."

In 1934, the Queen's contest began. "Just at dusk," Queen Lois recalls, "when the outline of the Cascades was still visible, there was an earth-shaking explosion, a sudden display of bursting skyrockets, the raising of the flag on the top of the arch while some one sang the 'Star Spangled Banner'. The arch lit up in a breath-taking blaze of color accompanied by the roar of an estimated 10,000 spectators along the river banks."

Excerpts from the Deschutes Pioneer Gazette

"The arch was used the first time in the year I was the Queen. They must have some expert technicians that did the lighting. The lighting constantly changed. It was really something to see. In the early days, they would have the floats floating freely in the water and down the river. It was an effort to keep the floats in the main channel. They would have some boys swimming along, pushing or pulling. Then they would get them all stacked up at the bottom. They would bring them all back up the river before the night time fell. In later years, they built a boom down the river and had it attached with electric plugs, I guess. So each float was lighted as it went down the river. It was really beautiful.

One year they had a float of George Washington crossing the Delaware in a little row boat. They fixed the row boat so it looked like there was snow all over it. Well, this was cotton batting. Apparently, George was a smoker because suddenly, there was smoke rolling up from the float. I think George had presence of mind to put it out. At least he didn't burn the thing!"

Lois Maker Gumpert

"It was on the Fourth of July. It even got so successful they put bleachers and sold reserved seats on the bleachers. It got so cold. People would come out wrapped in blankets and everything to try and keep warm. When the water pageant was goin', I would rent a big tank and put it up in front of the grocery store. I'd fill it full of ice and fill it full of watermelon. Then I prayed for hot weather. You don't sell watermelon in cold weather. So, we had speakers out there and music out there. Most of the time, I sold 'em out completely but time after time after time on the 30th of June it'd be cold."

Rolie Anderson

"They had some wonderful fire works just about towards the end of the line up. The downtown merchants furnished the fire works. They shot them off on the Drake Park side of the river. They experimented and one year they got a couple of floats on fire. And that was kind of a disaster but they got it out. The fire works landed on the floats but they were floating down the river and the river had lots of water so it wasn't really as bad as it seems.

They had famous people there. They had Burl Ives, I think, one year with his singing. The people would come down and sit on the bank of the river and, God it was cold out there. This was the July 4th celebration — but this was Bend and it was cold. People would bring blankets down with them. That's the way it is still — really cold."

Keith & Donna Clark

The pageant was a success, no question. And its popularity continued through the thirties to World War II and after the war until 1965, with one exception in 1951, when Shevlin-Hixon shut down. Changing times, population pressures, different community attitudes, rampant commercialism, lack of volunteers - all contributed to the pageant's end. But there was nothing else quite like it anywhere in Oregon.

From Olga (Alt) Norcott as told to Janice Schock in 1983.

'Course there were lots of coyotes there in those days, too. I remember one time I was going from that far field over the rock pile and this darn coyote's following me, and he'd howl every once in awhile. I'd turn around and I could see him and I tell you, the hair on the back of my head stood up. Of course, I had my shovel that I always irrigated with, so I felt pretty brave. 'Course we had these few killer coyotes that would kill chickens and stuff, and that was the only time we ever shot coyotes was if they got in our chickens because we let our chickens run loose, especially earlier years. They'd sneak up there about daylight and get a chicken. But if you get that one killer coyote, then the others didn't bother.

Even the Post Office Moved

Lois Gumpert
From a panel discussion moderated by Paul Reynolds on April 25, 2000

In the very beginning when the mills were first here, the loggers could walk to work. They lived in Bend and walked across the river where the timber was. Some of the single loggers lived in tents over on the west side of the river where most of them worked. As time went on the families started coming and they wanted to be all together. So the mills built houses for the people. When the timber was all cut in one area, they'd move the camps so they were always close to their work. In later years the engineers would mark out a map showing numbered lots. You could check out the map and put your name on any lot you wanted. Generally you'd decide on the basis of what scenery you wanted to look at from your house, Mt. Bachelor or something else.

The kitchen was always interesting to me at camp. They had a big kitchen. A whole car up on the railroad track. There were two cooks, a baker, two waitresses, and two dining cars, which were also up on the railroad tracks. They fed the single loggers. Those waitresses would serve the food and keep the place real clean. The floors were made of pine and the loggers had to come dressed to go to work so they'd have their calk boots on. Their boots chewed up the floors and the poor waitresses had to keep them scrubbed, which was quite a chore with that wood chewed up. They never ever let the food get cold on the table and would replace a dish immediately if it was cold. The loggers expected plenty of food and they needed it because they worked so hard.

About five o'clock in the morning they would hit a triangle that called the men to breakfast. They had a huge metal bowl in the kitchen that was on a stand. The cooks mixed the hot cakes in that and they used an ax handle for a stirrer. Of course it was brand new, and it was sterile. Whoever made the lunches laid the bread all out on a large metal top table and spread melted butter on it with a paintbrush. They'd paint the whole works and then added the filling. On the way out the door after breakfast, the men would pick up their lunch, which they called a nosebag. Some of them would tie their nosebag onto a tree, if their work was close to it, so that the squirrels didn't get into it.

There was a pie rack in the kitchen and they would have 30 or 40 pies in it. It took all that for one day and the baker did all that baking including the bread. One time they lost their second cook, who was the baker, and they hired a new one. He made delightful things like chocolate eclairs, cream puffs and elegant pastries. However the loggers weren't used to that and it wasn't long 'til he was on his way

Our post office had to move when the camp moved. Now in order to move your post office it seems you had to notify Washington that you were going to move to a certain place, on a certain day, at a certain hour so all the mail routes would converge in the right place. I was the Postmaster, so I started writing to the Postmaster General about having to move the post office. Unfortunately, I couldn't tell him what time we would move. You never quite knew when that was going to happen. Just a short time before it was time to go, they'd come and say, well we're going to be moving you in a week or so.

Under the circumstances, I had quite a correspondence with the office of the Postmaster General. We wrote back and forth because no one there could understand why a post office was going to move from Deschutes County into Klamath County. They had never heard of such a thing. It took reams of letters back and forth to the government to get permission to move the post office. After a year or so, I finally got permission to move, but before it came through, I had visions of sitting there among a pile of mail sacks with no post office and no patrons because the post office would be gone.

Lois (Maker) Gumpert, b.1914 in Prineville, lived her early years in logging camps near the area that became Sunriver. She was Queen of the 2nd Water Pageant in 1934. She was the postmaster of Shevlin for 10 years. Lois, her husband Ray and three children moved to Bend in 1948 where she worked in the office at Kenwood Elementary and Cascade Junior High. She continues to enjoy living a wonderful life in Bend.

Water in the Flumes and Not a Drop to Waste
Mary Griffith Scott

I was born on a farm near McMinnville, Yamhill County, Oregon and came to Bend in Central Oregon as a teenager in the early 30s to spend some time with my Uncle Charles and Aunt Clare Griffith. My uncle loved this country east of the Cascades and from him I learned it was very different than the area I grew up in; wide open spaces where water preservation was a must if one expected a crop to grow.

While my uncle worked at the mill, agriculture was his real interest and he worked diligently to get irrigation water to all the dry farms in Deschutes and Jefferson County. He went to Salem with his plea for monies to build the reservoirs for water storage from the melting snows. When this all came to be, the farms blossomed and produced in profusion.

I made many early morning trips to the farm east of Bend at Gosney and Arnold Market Roads with Uncle Charles. The hired men at the ranch always saddled a horse for me, though sometimes it was one too spirited for my "style." I'd complain, but Uncle

Charlie would say, "You just as well get up there and ride him - just remember, he already knows your scared of him." He always had plans for the day and they usually included a short ride across a big flat area, which is now the Deschutes County Landfill.

One of the chores I remember was riding out to check the leaks in the irrigation ditches, which were wooden flumes. Being in a country where the big industry was lumber, the material for those flumes was right at hand. The wooden flumes took constant care and mending. Dried roots from plants and weeds that grew there could be packed in smaller holes where they took on moisture and expanded to stop the leaks. As you rode along the flume there would be stacks of wood from time to time and we would use those to fix the bigger leaks.

I noticed as we rode across the desert, whenever we met anyone on horseback, each one would tip his hat and say, "Howdy." I'd ask, "Who was that man?" Often my uncle didn't know, but he always guessed their head of water was short too and they were looking to find out why.

I've lived in Bend most of my life and still say I wouldn't live anyplace else. Spending time with my uncle when I was young taught me to appreciate that water is a precious resource. I learned early on not to let it run wastefully on a sidewalk or anywhere else. Then and now, we needed it all to make our crops grow.

Mary (Griffith) Scott was born in Yamhill County, Oregon and moved to Central Oregon in 1934. She was a chef at area restaurants as well as helped her husband build custom homes.

Give me a young man in whom there is something of the old, and an old man in whom there is something of the young. Guided so, a man may grow old in body but never in mind.

Cicero

Sheep Tales

The Deschutes area was a prime area for sheepmen and herders. This area was considered as posh. It was less rugged than most areas where sheep were run. Sheepherders who came here from Idaho never wanted to return to that state. The reason was that here all the camps were accessible by roads and life was easier.

Supplies did not have to be delivered by a camp-tender with packhorses. Instead, camp-tenders drove supplies to the herders and hauled water to the bands of sheep with vehicles. Herders stayed in trailers instead of teepees or canvas wall tents.

Although there were coyotes in the area, there wasn't the problem with bears coming into the herds and killing the sheep like piñatas. Bears in other northern states would come into the bands and go on killing sprees. Sometimes the bear would kill 40 to 60 sheep for sport. But, not here.

Shaniko was considered the capitol of the sheep world and the railroad depot was there. Huge bands were driven by horseback to Shaniko to be shipped by rail.

Sheep were wintered on the desert. In the spring, the sheep would be divided into bands and driven to summer grazing in the mountains where they would range over as much as 40,000 acres. A sheepherder stayed with his band of sheep with his dogs 24 hours a day seven days a week. They did not get any days off until the band was sold or they quit. Then, many would stay in town until their money was gone.

Sheep were big business from about the 1900's to just after World War II. That was when synthetics (polar fleeces) were developed. Synthetics replaced the use of wool. The government no longer had the incentives for wool production and herd numbers dwindled.

"When we first moved in, we didn't have a phone yet. When my second daughter was about to be born, I had to go across the street to the neighbors to call the doctor's. While I was standing over there, another band of sheep came through and the young girl said, "What are you going to do?" I said, "Well, I'm sure not going to go out in the middle of that band of sheep. I'm going to stand here until it goes through. I think she was afraid I was going to have a baby on her lawn. So, I just waited until the sheep passed and we went to the hospital. We got to the hospital in time!"

Evelyn Sather

"The sheepherders worked a little in the winter. But it seemed like they'd close it down some in the winter. In the summer, a sheepherder would go out there, and man, you lived out there. You had to be in constant control of the sheep. If a straggler was getting away from you, you had to be there. You had to be there twenty-four hours a day. So, they'd come into Bend and let their hair down, raise some hell."

Bruno Baer

"One of the things that always stuck in my mind was Jack Shumway, a sheep rancher who lived in Alfalfa. He would herd the sheep from Alfalfa up into Three Creeks area for the summer. He had the contract to run them up there. When they'd trail them through Bend, it would take four hours or longer. They had three bands which is 6,000 head of sheep. They would divide them up in three or four different bunches, you couldn't handle all of 'em at once. They would literally stall. You wouldn't be able to get around them. Most of the time, you'd just have to set until they cleared. And it was up to nearly everybody to keep the sheep out of your yard so they wouldn't eat the flowers and all that stuff. I can remember up there where the fancy houses are up on the hill (Awbrey Butte), they kept them there overnight many times. That was one of the places they would stop and let the sheep rest. This was every year for years and years and years."

Joe Kentner

"We used to ride horse back out to the east to do chores on my uncle's ranch. Very often there would be a huge herd of sheep bedded down there for the night. The shepherds quietly had their breakfast at the chuck wagon and then sent their well-trained dogs to waken the sheep. Uncle Charlie told me you don't ask a sheepman how many sheep he has. He would say four or five herds. It was sorta like asking him what his bank account balance was."

Mary Griffith Scott

"Today is ours. What do we fear!
Today is ours. We have it here!
Let's treat it kindly, that it may
Wish, at least, with us to stay.
Banish business, banish sorrow.
To the gods belongs tomorrow.

From Today is Ours
By Abraham Cowley (1616-1667)

Bruno Baer

Crazy Times at the Waldorf Café
Bruno Baer

My dad and mom got married at 7 o'clock in the morning in Frazee, Minnesota just so they could be on their way to Bend, Oregon that same day. Dad worked as a timekeeper for the Shevlin-Hixon Company back in the late '20s and early '30s until 1934 when he bought a bar called the Waldorf Café. It was where the present day U.S. Bank parking lot is on Bond Street. He had it for 39 years, from 1934 to 1973.

When me and my two brothers were kids, we worked at the bar. Seems like we always got my dad in trouble. My older brother Bill was constantly pulling tricks. For instance, my dad always started pouring drinks at 4 o'clock in the afternoon. Bill knew when he was going to pour and he'd wait until my dad would go into the walk-in refrigerator to get pop for the mix. Then he would follow Dad and put one of those great big, long construction nails in the lock so that he couldn't get out. Usually Bill would let him out within five to ten minutes, but one day he forgot and walked away and left Dad in there for forty-five minutes or an hour. When he finally remembered and opened it up and looked in, there was Dad way in the back among those old wooden Coke boxes, breaking 'em up, trying to start a fire. He was so mad at my brother he yelled, "Bill, I'm gonna get you," and they both took off runnin'.

Front row from left: The first man could be Mr. Leverette, Bill Baer, Ross Farnham, Superintendent of the courthouse project, E.E. Varco. Second row: Mr. Triplett, Mr. Smith, do not know who the next two are; Chris Allen, 1938.

Back in the '40s and '50s, the Irish sheepherders and the loggers and what construction workers there were, made Bend, Oregon. I mean, that's how you got your living. And you had to cater to them. We had some sheepherders that would come in from the range some, oh, probably a couple months before Christmas and they kept to the bar until spring. They trusted my dad because he was honest. They'd come in and give him whatever they had, $1500 or $2000. And then they'd just drink off of that until their money was gone.

The Irish sheepherders, for some reason, would always bring their freaks to my dad. One time one of them brought in a black ram that had five legs. Dad held it for 2 or 3 days and finally got rid of it. Another time, when I was about 10 or 12 years old, somebody brought a monkey to us. That monkey climbed up on top of a car and without thinking I reached up to pick it off the roof. He grabbed my fingers, put 'em in his mouth and bit 'em. I got away from that quick and we gave the monkey back.

One thing about a restaurant and bar, if the bar is doing all right then the restaurant isn't. Or if the restaurant is doing all right, then the bar isn't. It just seems like you're losing money on one of 'em all the time. My mom worked the restaurant next door to the bar. She'd go down there about 3:30 or 4:00 in the morning and wouldn't get out until about 12:30 or 1:00 the next morning. While she was working, my dad would be at the other extreme, playing golf or just socializing, or whatever. Naturally, my mother would raise a little bit of hell with him, and I don't blame her. Management wise, I think she was a little bit superior. My dad was smart, but she had the business sense. Mom worked real hard in that restaurant and my sisters Barbara and Janice helped her out whenever they could. That restaurant was far more work than the bar ever was.

While my dad had the bar, we lived at 974 Riverside, which is just a block downtown from the old post office. It's a beautiful white Spanish house. He had that built. I lived there all my life. It's kind of funny. You'd think we were in the farm area or something because I had chickens, rabbits, and even a Shetland pony there.

Mrs. Dacy was the County Clerk and she was my dad's next door neighbor. She complained because, when my dad went out of business in 1973, he brought everything conceivable from the Waldorf home. He brought the spittoons, he brought the steel rail that you put your feet on, and he brought the urinals. He even brought the bar home. It was about seventy feet long and was the longest stainless steel bar in Oregon.

My dad had a flair for good humor. I'll never forget the time he went to church and Father Bill was up there. He had our two Great Danes with him and they started barking and howling. Finally, Father Bill had to stop Mass and ask Bill Baer if he'd take his dogs home. And then another time he and old Pat Cashman - a good Irish guy who had the Cashman Clothier - tried to play a game with one another at 11 o'clock mass. Came collection time Pat Cashman put in one dollar, and he looked at my dad. And my dad put in two dollars. And then Pat put in three. And my dad, he didn't mean to, but he dropped a couple of fives and one or two tens and a twenty. And then he tried to get the collection guy to give him back his money. But the collection guy just took it and looked at my dad and Pat Cashman, and old Pat was laughing his head off.

For years Dad was really involved with the community. He was County Commissioner several times, but when he campaigned in later years he didn't get anywhere. All the old timers who were behind him had died off or moved out of the area, but the stories about Dad and the crazy times at the Waldorf live on.

Bruno Baer, b. 1937 in Bend, Oregon. He was a member of the last class to graduate from the original high school on Wall St. and has lived in Bend most of his life. His father William J. Baer, Sr., owned the Waldorf Café on Bond Street and was a county commissioner in the 1940s and 50s.

From Sheep to Cars
Evelyn Sather

We moved to 8th Street in 1940. My husband saw an ad and bought four lots, paid $50 a lot. My husband built this house himself. We lived in it during the building process.

About the time we got our lawn in, one morning about 5 o'clock, we'd hear these bells coming along and here would come, oh, probably several thousand sheep. And so, we'd have to get out and keep the sheep off the lawn. There were regular shepherds with their dogs but the lawn was nice and green and the sheep wanted to eat it.

I think they were coming from a ranch in Madras. They went all the way up to the foothills in the mountains. They brought the sheep down once or twice in the spring. They didn't bring them back in the fall. I don't know what they did with them in the fall. Maybe they just sold them off up there.

When we first moved here there weren't many houses. The neighbors used to help each other build their houses. The house on the other side of us was built by a man who was a cook at a restaurant downtown. He was building a replica of his home in Tennessee. It's got a big front porch, you know, where I think they sat in rockers. That house is still there.

The area all around here was rocks and sagebrush and stray cats. There was a little road and people would drive along that little road and dump off their cats in the rocks. So there were lots of stray cats.

I remember we had two pine trees in our back yard. I had my clothesline stretched between them. Well, one day, all of a sudden I heard this "thud". There was this little, old doctor called Dr. Tom. He was used to taking a short cut behind our house. Well, he didn't see my clothesline so he ran into it with his car, and he was so surprised.

We had a great big garden. We even had chickens. My husband was going to prove he could grow anything. We had corn, potatoes, carrots and peas, and green beans which mostly froze.

They'd make it sometimes but we'd have killing frost, you know, almost every month of the year.

The neighbor used to raise goats for the milk. When they sold that house they thought they'd be funny and tell the new owner that he could even have pigs if he wanted to out here. So, he did. He had the first and only pig in the neighborhood.

When my daughters were growing up, there were lots of children for them to play with. There was really no traffic on 8th street. You could play off in the middle the street, practically, until the sheep came, of course. The kids would just run back and forth up the street. There were no streetlights.

There were all these little family grocery stores that you could walk to. So, if you wanted groceries you could easily walk. We used to walk pushing baby buggies to the grocery store and back.

Then during World War II, when they had Camp Abbott and they had the maneuvers here, then we had a black quartermasters corp. bivouacked across on the southeast corner of Norton and 8th. That was when the military was segregated. And those men would drill up and down in front of our house. It was such fun to watch them, they had such rhythm and cadence. Dust and all, they just drilled away.

After the war, we started getting more houses so, of course, there was more traffic. They paved the street because it was what they called a "farm to market road".

There were a lot of young families moving in to start with. In this particular neighborhood we'd have sort of block parties. It was just a friendly neighborhood. Everybody had a gate or path through to their house and just went back and forth. Now there are just fences and no gates. Everyone's fenced off. It's not a neighborhood like it once was.

So, I guess you'd have to say that 8th street went from driving sheep down it to driving cars.

Evelyn Sather was born in 1916 in a log cabin in Minnesota. She moved to Bend in 1938. She has always lived on 8th Street and had a career as a teacher.

97

Sailing
Leonard Peoples

My dad loved to sail. He'd sail anything, anywhere, anytime. He built all his boats. He worked at the Shevlin-Hixon Company so it was easy to get the lumber. This was in the '20s and '30s. In Central Oregon, you couldn't buy a boat if you wanted to.

We started going to Elk Lake around 1931 when I was about three. We spent every summer up there. We rented a cabin with my mother's sister and her husband and two boys. It was basically two bedrooms and kitchen downstairs and a balcony. All the kids slept upstairs in the balcony. My mother died in 1937 and my aunt and uncle built their own cabin up there. So we rented the cabin until 1941 when Dad married Margaret Kane, the girl in the cabin next door. And then we moved next door, you see. My stepmother's father, Charles Kane, helped build that cabin. And when it was finished the owner decided to sell it and Kane bought it for 125 dollars and a Model T Ford.

There've been basically no new cabins on the lake since about 1940. I guess there must be 35 or 40 cabins. And we knew most of them. The Veatch's had the cabin two down from us. John Veatch was a good friend of my brother Sam. John and Betsy Veatch now live in Bend. And next door to them was the Cleveland's. Nancy Cleveland is still in Bend. She married one of the Cleveland brothers. They were a little bit older than me. Of course, I was the youngest of our clan so everybody else seems old. I remember, we'd have campfires down in one of the campgrounds by the resort on weekends. Sing songs and burn marshmallows.

Dad built his first boat here in 1920. And he got quite a few people interested in sailing. In 1937, he built a Geary 18, which was designed for people to build at home. It was a good boat. He did get people to build them and they got a fleet. In fact, six guys from Brooks-Scanlon went in together and in one winter they built six hulls. Since Tom Brooks, one of the builders, lived on

Drake Road, the boats were named Drake I through VI. And they drew lots as to who would get number one and number two and so forth. Because as they went along their workmanship had gotten better. Everybody wanted the sixth one. They started sailing those boats and raced against each other. You had to establish handicaps for the races. You'd race all summer to establish the handicaps. I was the youngest so I got to sail Dad's twelve-foot scow, the Wild Kitten. And of course, it was the smallest and slowest boat. We'd start the regatta with the slowest boat first and each boat in turn according to its time handicap. I remember one regatta; Jim Hosmer and I were sailing. And we had our fifteen-minute handicap. And we were off and flying. And we had great winds and we led the fleet the whole race until about 200 yards or so from the finish line. And I sailed into a hole in the wind. The other boats were behind us and they could see we had no wind. So they sailed around this thing and we were dead in the water. There wasn't a thing we could do.

We'd spend the whole summer up there. We got home just in time to get a haircut and go back to school. That was about the only time we saw town. But we had a good time. I still have a sailboat and we still go up there to sail.

Dad built an iceboat. We did most of our ice boating on Tumalo Reservoir. They'd put about two or three feet of water in it in the fall and let it freeze. And before the snows came we could skate on it. And it was really kind of nice because it was probably about a mile in diameter and there was a lot of skating. The iceboat, it was flat-bottomed. And it had probably 1x6 sides. The hull would be about three feet wide and maybe ten feet long. And then it had three runners. Two set on about a 2x8 plank that was probably ten feet wide to give the boat stability. And one runner in front to steer with. And then he made the mast and the sail. It's possible, in sailing, to go faster than the wind. And with the ice boat there's not much friction or resistance. So you go pretty fast. I don't know how fast we would go but it would seem much faster because you'd be less than a foot off the ice. You'd go bumping along over the rough ice. With so little ice out there on the reservoir, it got pretty rough pretty soon. There were lots of people ice skating out there. The reservoir was big enough for everybody and they kind of accepted it, as we'd sail by.

And we also had a skate sail. A sail that you held when you ice-skated. It was a triangular sail. The spars were in the form of a 'T' with the leading edge, the vertical spar in front. I would say it was about six feet long. And the trailing spar, which was the center part of the 'T', was about eight or ten feet long. And you would sail with your body downwind from the sail. You were like the main mast. You'd hold the sail with your two hands, one hand in front and one hand behind. And just go for it. When you got done, you'd let go with your rear hand and let the sail just drag in the wind and you could turn around. It seemed like you were goin' faster than the iceboats, but of course you weren't. But it sure seemed like it. It sure was fun. I don't remember anybody else ever building another ice boat or skate sail.

Leonard Peoples, b. 1927 in Bend. After attending local schools, Leonard developed a career in mechanical engineering, which led him to Portland, the East Coast and South Africa. He has returned to his hometown to live.

Sisters, Oregon

Rave Reviews for Indoor Plumbing

Dale, Marilyn, and Hanna Elkin

Sisters, Oregon was a very small town when Dale Elkin moved there in 1933 at the age of two. "There were wooden sidewalks and no street signs," Dale recalls. "The streets were all named but there never were any signs, so nobody knew where they were. They just got a mailbox number. In 1941 the Works Projects Administration (WPA) put in the concrete sidewalks. The sidewalks are stamped at the ends with WPA 1941." Dale and his wife Marilyn helped put the street signs up in 1964.

By all accounts, Sisters was a great place to be a kid. "We boys used to make stilts," Dale recounts. "We'd go down to the sawmill and get edgings and make stilts. We'd build roads out in the woods too. We'd build wagons and go loggin' and we'd have loggin' roads, and we used to run hoops. We used to make sling shots with a single rubber band and shoot arrows with 'em. There weren't enough hours in the day for us when I was a kid.

We'd get wheelbarrows and wagons and hammers and we'd go with my grandmother to the dump. It was about a half-mile. In

101

those days oranges, grapefruit, apples, and everything came in wooden crates. We'd tear those crates all apart and get the nails. Back home my grandmother would help us build squirrel cages and rabbit hutches. We didn't have to buy toys to entertain us. We stayed pretty busy."

Hanna Elkin, Dale's sister-in-law, remembers Sisters was a quiet place. She remembers her activities as a teenager in Sisters. She moved there in 1937 at the age of 18. "I used to borrow the bicycle of the son of the people I worked for. My friend Martha and I would ride up and down the streets. At the Sisters Hotel Martha and I would charge a sundae every now and then. That's about the way everybody did. Everything was charged 'til the family got paid. I think they had a payday and a draw day. We always charged all of our groceries 'til the end of the month."

Hanna recalls, "At the gym at school we used to go roller-skating. And if we could find somebody with a car we went to a show either in Redmond or Bend. It didn't take too long to get to Bend, especially if Homer (her future husband) was driving."

When asked what she misses of the old days, Hanna says, "I don't know. I guess mostly that I was younger and had more fun." Asked what she misses least, she quickly exclaims, "Outdoor privies! We never had a bathroom in Sisters, only an outhouse. Our first indoor bathroom was in Bend about 1950."

Marilyn agreed. "After we moved to Sisters, the house wasn't done yet. Neither was the outhouse. We were playing hide-and-seek one night and I ran into the outhouse. I was going to hide in there but the front wasn't built in yet, just the seat. I slid right down into the hole."

To which Dale added with a twinkle in his eye, "I knew there had been a problem somewhere back then!"

Hanna (Wagner) Elkin, b.1919 in Minnesota. She moved to the Sisters area in 1937. During World War II she worked in Portland as a lady welder. She was the cook at Bend High for 22 years. Dale and Marilyn (Morris) Elkin both grew up in Sisters. Dale worked in the lumber industry. Marilyn served the Madras schools as a cook for 18 years.

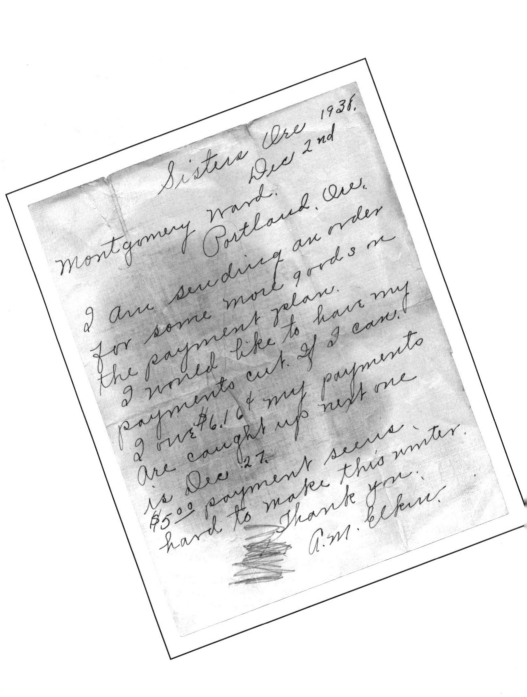

Sisters Ore 1931.
Dec 2nd
Montgomery Ward.
Portland. Ore.

I am sending an order
for some more goods on
the payment plan.
I would like to have my
payments cut. If I can.
I owe $6.16 t my payments
are caught up next one
is Dec 27.
$5.00 payment seems
hard to make this winter.
Thank you.
A.M. Elkins.

The Smell of the Pines
Keith Clark

They called it the "Great Depression" and if that doesn't scare you, well that's good. There were a lot of people lost jobs, businesses.

The big mills made a point though of not shutting down. They knew if they did, they were gone. You talk about Bend, and you talk about these mills, they were really great big monsters. It was a full time industry for the people in Bend for, gosh, I don't know how long.

The Deschutes provided natural mill flow. There were a lot of pines. I don't know how many, but miles of pines. The people who were in charge of the mills just came at the river and cut those trees so that they could float them down to where they could get 'em out easy.

These mills were kind of a godsend. Their harvesting of the trees provided lots of raw material. And then the community was built by people who were really interested in building something along with the mill section. They wanted to see other things come in too.

Everybody really counted on each other, but it was tough. My dad tried to stay out of the mill during the Depression. He was a line-man who worked for Pacific Power and Light and he put in, oh wow, long, long hours. Soon as I got big enough to go and stand around underneath, where he could drop something heavy on me, well I'd be out there with him. He gave me a different perspective — I must have some value or they would have downed me with one of those big heavy transformers. Most of those deals were installations of new transformers. My dad was able to work all the time.

You know, I've never quite forgotten the smell of those trees and the timber — clean and clear. I can remember the smell of the trees. There were big, old pines. The mills were running and that was more pine smell. And then the cafes and restaurants had trees right outside the windows. So did the old Pilot Butte Inn. And for me, that pine scent still brings back memories.

"We Didn't Have It Too Bad"
Donna Clark

By the time the Depression hit in '29, I was 3 years old. As far as my family was concerned, we didn't have it too bad. There were just Wayne and me with my folks.

I had some grandparents that lived down at Powell Butte. We could go out there and help with the potato harvest once a year, and sometimes I'd help my grandmother pick berries and fruit and vegetables, and she'd send some of that home with us. And we'd help churn sometimes. I thought that was great; I could churn the milk! My grandparents didn't have a dairy, so they brought their milk into Redmond and sold it down there at what is now Ace Hardware. The money from the milk was just about enough for my grandparents to get the special things that they weren't raising, like maybe dried beans, flour, sugar — those kinds of things.

My dad's family came to Bend from Colorado, and previous to that had come from Russia. Dad was 17 when he went to work in the mill about 1922. He worked all the way through the Depression. If I remember right, he started out as any younger person would, sweeping up stuff and scraps. Eventually, he got into loading trucks and then into sawing.

Most of the mills never shut down. They made sure everybody got work. Very limited, it had to be. One month my father got a check for $8. That wasn't considered a lot in those days.

Before the Depression hit, the mills helped in giving a discounted price to people who were building houses here in Bend. My folks, Joe and Mary Werner, built a shack in 1926 and later turned it into a garage when they built the bigger house in the early '30s.

My folks were so good. Mom would sew our clothing. They would tell us kids, "Now take care of your clothes and don't walk in the mud or the puddles with your shoes 'cause we can't get you another pair. But when you outgrow these, why then you'll get some new shoes." Which they did, they saved it up, whatever they could. Shoes cost probably somewhere between $3 and $4.

They would make a garden. She would can foods and Dad would go fishing. Sometimes she'd go with him. Didn't have to go very far 'cause they were just a few blocks away from the Deschutes River.

At that time the entertainment that was going on was playing cards and visiting, having coffee with your friends. They both loved coffee, and maybe they'd have some kind of canned fruit or something for dessert. While the adults played cards, we kids would go in the back room and have a talent show.

The times were tough and our pleasures were simple, but my memories of those Depression days are good.

Keith and Donna (Werner) Clark are native to Bend. Keith had a career in education, finally retiring from COCC. Keith and Donna have co-authored many books and served as the editors of the Deschutes Pioneers' Gazette for many years. They live in Redmond.

How It Snowed, How It Snowed, How It Snowed!

Lester Joseph Kentner

Back then when it snowed. . . .

When it snowed, they would take Norton Street and block it off. There was a pretty good sized hill there and the kids would use that to sled down. They blocked off Awbrey Heights too. People simply weren't allowed to go up and down that with any kind of vehicle. It was strictly for the kids the whole entire time winter was here. Lots of snow and the kids just used it. Troy Field is downtown by St. Francis school, and they would flood it with a fire truck or hydrants and keep it frozen for the kids to ice skate on.

To get rid of the snow downtown they would blow it into dump trucks to get it off the streets. We lived at 346 East Fifth Street and there was an alley between Clay & DeKalb. They would blow that snow down that alley and it would be so high that you couldn't even see the rooftops of our neighbors. We'd hollow it out and make a fort in there. It would be about fifteen feet wide and twenty to twenty-five feet long, and it would stay that way the whole winter.

Sometimes they dumped snow in the Deschutes too. They'd go down past the Pine Tavern, back up to the Deschutes River and just dump. We'd have icebergs floating in the Deschutes River as far as you could see. Another place they would dump it in the river was off the older bridge that was down below where Pioneer Park is now.

Back then when it snowed, it snowed and it'd stay cold. You didn't have days like we do now, nice days and a few inches of snow. It really snowed back then.

Lester Joe Kentner, b. 1940 in Bend, attended school in Tumalo and Redmond. He established several small businesses including Bend Lock and Key and he raised and sold parakeets and canaries wholesale. He has restored 144 cars over 40 years as a hobby.

Memories of Birchard's Neighborhood Grocery

Fern (Birchard) Barnett and Hazel (Birchard) LeBlanc

Before the days of VISA and MasterCard there were charge account books at neighborhood grocery stores like the Birchard's. Veva and Earl purchased their little store on East Third Street in 1942. Like so many others of that era, it had attached living quarters. At that time East Third Street was a state-designated truck route through Bend.

Initially Veva ran the store alone while Earl worked first at the Shevlin-Hixon Mill and later as a security guard at Camp Abbott after it was vacated near the end of WW II. Later they ran it together. At first the store was very small, but in 1946 Earl, with the help of a neighbor, built a larger building for it and the small, original one became a storeroom.

There was a buzzer over the door, that rang in the living quarters when a customer came in. Veva usually dashed in herself to wait on the customer, but if she was busy in the home and the girls were home, she would send one of them with the instructions to call her if it was a large order or a tobacco purchase. She never, ever sold alcohol in her store.

From 7:00 AM to 10:00 PM, seven days a week, every week, the Birchards ran their store. They rarely took a vacation. Even after the 10:00 PM closing, if a neighbor needed something and the house lights were on, they knew they could knock on the living room door and one of the Birchards would take them into the store.

Their daughter Hazel remembers the WW II Army soldier convoy trucks stopping across the street in a long line and her Mom calling to her to come dip ice cream cones. It seemed

Original Birchard's Grocery, 1942

108

Mrs. Earl Birchard at counter, Nov. 1973

an endless line of khaki uniforms waiting for their five cent cones on a hot day!

Her sister Fern recalled their Mom as the neighborhood psychiatrist. She listened attentively to personal problems of her faithful customers, and offered her "Dear Abby" advice.

A wooden box sat on the store counter with the charge account books. If a customer couldn't pay the full bill on payday, that was fine. They were allowed to pay what they could then and to catch up when they could. Credit was always extended to people with families. On occasion, Veva even acted as a pawnbroker. She allowed a reasonable amount of credit for groceries and held a personal item, such as a watch, until it could be reclaimed.

Veva and Earl were very proud that their customers, who were also their friends and neighbors, were honest people who rarely failed to pay a charged bill or to return to pick up an item held for groceries. No one ever attempted to rob the neighborhood store, although there were a few incidents of sticky-fingered youths. Usually they were unaware of those transgressions until the perpetrators came back as adults to pay for a candy bar or cigarettes and apologize for their youthful action.

Fern also recalls the Sunday morning that their Mom decided to take an hour off and attend church services with the family. However, rushing about to get ready, she completely forgot to lock the store door. She returned to find money all over the counter. The honest customers had shopped and paid, proving as they had often said that it was a great neighborhood for running a grocery store.

Veva and Earl watched a generation of their customers grow up. Some came back as adults to say hello and ask if they remembered them as children, buying penny candy from the little glass case next to the counter. When the time came to sell in 1972 she was reluctant to let the store go but Earl was ready to close the door on that era. But like those long gone cash registers, the memories of those days ring on for their daughters and the customers who remember the Birchard's store.

Hazel (Birchard) LeBlanc and Fern (Birchard) Barnett were both born in Wapinitia, Oregon. The moved to Bend in 1930 where they lived on Greenwood Ave. and attended Bend schools. They both continue to live in Bend.

Twin Mountain Muffins

1/4 cup shortening

1/4 cup sugar

1/2 teaspoon salt

4 teaspoons baking powder

1 cup milk

2 cup flour

1 egg

Cream the shortening; add the sugar and egg well beaten; sift in the baking powder and the flour, and add to the first mixture, alternating with milk. Bake in greased pan 25 minutes or so. 350 degrees.

Dorothy McClain remembers recipes from when she was a girl. Recipes from little girls were featured each month in a farm magazine. Dorothy remembers eagerly waiting for the new recipes and stories to come out.

To know how to grow old is the master work of wisdom, and one of the most difficult chapters in the great art of living.

Henri Amiel

September 1948, McKenzie Pass

Weekends Were For Smoking Fish and Picking Potatoes
Nettie Harris

In September, 1948, we moved to Bend from Rainier, Minnesota. First we headed for the coast, then traveled south from Seaside and decided to go inland at Florence. We were driving a brand new 1-ton orange Chevrolet truck over the old McKenzie highway. With that big truck and all those curves, we just took our time and enjoyed the beautiful country.

We couldn't find a place to rent in Bend but we found a little mickey mouse house that the fellow who owned it wanted to sell, so we bought it for $2,600. It's still there at 502 Arizona St. down by the railroad tracks. Part of the mill is still there too. There were 2 big sawmills then — Shevlin-Hixon and Brooks-Scanlon. They hauled logs day and night and at night you could hear the big log trains going by. We stayed there a lot of years. I wanted to buy some homes, nice ones, real reasonable, but I never could get my husband to move out of that house.

Weekends we did a lot of camping. The roads were just little narrow, sandy things. One road, one truck or one car. You'd look behind and the dust would be so thick, just flying back of us. It was just awful. We camped at all the lakes we could think of up in the Cascade Mountains. The kids would just sleep out in the open under the stars. We'd leave Friday night when my husband came home from work and came back on Sunday night 'cause he'd have to go back to work again and the kids had to go to school.

We all loved to fish and we caught lots with our big bamboo poles. My husband Bill liked to smoke them. He made a smokehouse out of an old refrigerator that we had standing along the side of the fence in our yard. They'd go hunting too. They'd get deer, and ducks, and pheasants. You didn't have to go very far back then. In those days everybody was on the poor side, you know, strugglin' and workin', but those were fun days.

There were a lot of beer places in Bend in '48. Down there on Minnesota Avenue they had beer places everywhere. Because of the mills there were lots of single men in town. Over there where Eddie's Canton is now, there used to be a big enormous rooming house with a lot of rooms and stuff. Then where the Eagles is, they had these places, where they . . . you know. We're talking about them red light houses. When the railroad fellars would come into town they'd stay overnight or something. Bond Street was the place with most of the beer places and those other kind of houses. Wall Street had Penney's, Sears & Roebuck, Montgomery Wards, a jewelry store, two theaters, and eating places, and that big furniture store owned by Bill Healy.

Work was hard then. I waitressed lots of different places. There were small restaurants everywhere and they did mostly home style cookin. To make extra money I would pick turkey feathers off of turkeys and pick potatoes. We would go out towards Sisters just up the hill from Tumalo to pick potatoes. Gee, we used to have beautiful potatoes.

The first time I worked like crazy because they were giving seven cents for a 60 pound sack. I must have picked 200 sacks the first day. And there were lots of potatoes laying around and we could take them home. The next day I couldn't get out of bed. My heavens, I'll tell ya, it was awful. Someone said that if I'd go out and do it again, I would get over it, and so I went back on Sunday and picked another 200 sacks. And they were right. I made $14 each day and I felt rich!

I could've bought into Bachelor for $25 in the early days but I didn't do it. That fellar, Bill Healy, called and asked if I wanted to. Oh gosh, money was so scarce then, but I could kick myself now for not doing it.

When we came to Oregon from Minnesota my husband was looking to work in the paper mills in North Bend. But North Bend was so small it wasn't on our map. Bend was on the map and we just assumed that North Bend was part of Bend. So you might say that we got here by accident. But it was a nice little town to live in, and we loved it.

Nettie (Ginter) Harris came to Bend in 1948 as a young woman from Minnesota. She worked as a housekeeper and waitress at the Greyhound Bus depot and other restaurants.

We opened Bend Poultry Company. The markets would call in the morning and tell us how many chickens and eggs to bring them. Bob & I would get up at 4 AM and go to the chicken ranches and buy the live chickens and eggs. We had two ladies that could candle 30 dozen eggs in just 15 minutes. They would hold up each egg to the light to check for blood, or to see if they were too old or if they had chickens in them. We did 300 chickens a day.

Wilma Lowe

Klondike Kate

Michael Houser
Associate Planner, Historic & Cultural Resources, Deschutes County

Born Kathleen Eloisa Rockwell in 1876, famed Central Oregonian "Klondike Kate or Aunt Kate" as the locals called her, left her Kansas home at the young age of 24 to join a dancing troop in Dawson, Alaska. An avid dancer, singer and actress, Kate quickly became know as the "Queen of the Yukon" and with her live-in boyfriend, Alexander Pantages, they started one of the nations greatest vaudeville theater chains.

Upon her retirement from show business, she left Alaska and settled in Central Oregon where she became one of Bend's most colorful citizens, and Central Oregon's first rockhound. She ranks today among the West's most legendary characters and her exploits in Alaska are known around the globe. She originally settled one mile north of Brothers and eventually moved into Bend, building a home at 231 NW Franklin Avenue (demolished in 1985). Locally she may be best remembered for her volunteer work with the Bend Fire Department and her unwavering need to help anyone less fortunate than her.

Klondike Kate

Bill Baer

I met Klondike Kate around 1943 when she came to my parents' house. She had been an entertainer up in Alaska and made quite a name for herself. At the time she was probably in her late 70's, but you could tell that she had been a pretty lady in her day. I was probably twelve or thirteen then and you could say I was curious and intrigued.

Kate was wearing an enormous amount of gold jewelry. She had a double stranded gold necklace with little chains hangin' down, and each of those had a gold nugget on the end. She had a bracelet similar to what we would call a charm bracelet. It, too, had little chains with little gold nuggets of different sizes on it, much like her necklace. Finally, she had a chain around her waist that featured the same little chains hanging down in front with gold nuggets on each of those. They were nuggets that people threw on the stage after she got through performing.

My brothers and sisters were not old enough to appreciate who she was, but I was right at the stage that I was peekin' around the corner. She motioned to me to come on out, and when I did she put her arm around me, took her bracelet off and put it in my hand. It was heavy, but the gold nuggets weren't what I thought gold nuggets would look like. You know what a Styrofoam ice chest looks like? Well, they looked like pieces of Styrofoam, but they were gold. I think she just wore it that one time to show it off for the family. That was pretty expensive stuff to be walkin' around town with.

She'd leave Bend and go to California and do a little entertaining in her later years. Kate started a home up here in Horse Ridge in the canyon. While they were building her house, the well dried up. Her response was to say that you can't live in a house that doesn't have water. So they just stopped work on it. Aunt Kate, as some people called her, came back into town and built on Franklin Street, behind the Catholic Church. The foundation was made out of river rock. The rest was made out of logs. It wasn't a big house but it was nice and I felt bad when they tore it down. They should have saved it; it was a landmark.

William J. Baer, b. 1934 in Bend, Oregon and attended Bend schools. He worked as a saw filer for 30 years for Brooks-Scanlon mills. His wife, Marilyn Waterman, also a native of Bend, was a past Water Pageant queen. His father owned the Waldorf Café on Bond Street and was a county commissioner in the 1940s and 50s.

My Mother's Apron

My Mother's old plain apron
Was a garment full and wide
It filled its humble mission
And a million more beside.

T'was made of six cent gingham
It was neither fine nor grand
Just a plain and simple pattern
Made by a busy hand.

It had a little cross-stitch
Along the bottom row
And two long strings that tied behind
In a hasty half-hitch bow.

It had no lace or ruffles
Nor pretty applique
But its simple home usefulness
Was an epic of the day.

T'was usto shoo the flies
T'was usto to wipe away tears
From weeping infant's eyes
T'was usto fill the kindling box

With chips of cobs or twigs
And tote the pesky weeds
From the garden to the pigs.
T'was usto snatch the hot kettles
When a pot rag was not at hand
To tighten on fruit jar lids
When winter stores were canned.
T'was usto gather garden stuff
And fruit from the hill
And many a goodly mess of greens
Did Mother's apron fill.

Her hands were sheltered from the gale
Beneat the sheltered fold
Any tiny feet nestled there
On mornings bleak and cold.

T'was a queenly garment
And Mother was a queen
As memory brings it back to me
T'was a noble thing I ween (think)

And when I wander at Heaven's throng
With robes so bright and fair
I'll say the old plain apron
Is what I want to wear.

This poem was given to Helen Rastovich by a friend. She has treasured it because it reminds her of her mother-in-law. It hangs on a wooden plaque in her home.

Ration Books, Victory Gardens and Forbidden Pleasures
Geordie Johnston

In the decade of the 1940's, when I was six to sixteen, we lived in Bend at 444 Riverside. We were the Emory and Rose Johnston family. Emory, our dad, was the District Maintenance Superintendent for the Oregon State Highway Department, while Rose was the housewife and mother to us three boys - Bob, Dick and me, Geordie.

Those were the war years in Bend - World War II. We took dimes to Reid School to buy savings stamps that we licked and placed in five and ten-dollar booklets which were saved 'for a rainy day'. There was rationing too during those years, and stamps were needed for butter, eggs, meat, sugar, gasoline, cigarette and tires - to help the war effort.

Camp Abbott sprung up south of Bend and Dad drove us out to park along the roadway and watch the war maneuvers - red against blue. When the soldiers were on leave, citizens of Bend gave up their homes to them and their visiting families.

Each Bend family who had a son or husband in the war displayed a blue flag in the window with a silver star. If the star turned to gold it meant that the family was 'one who gave'.

We kids had our own rag-tag army. Led by our 'lieutenant' Billy Niskanen (who later became one of our nation's foremost economists) we stealthily advanced up water-tank hill. I was a corporal, a squad leader. Some of us had canteen belts and other war paraphernalia. We all had sticks or BB guns for artillery. When we finally captured the hill, we stood there tall and triumphant, and using hand Morse code we had learned in scouting, signaled down to town that all was clear.

Almost everyone kept victory gardens during the war years. Ours was in the vacant lot just to the north of us. I can still picture the garden behind the raspberry bushes on the left. Mom and Dad grew potatoes, onions, carrots, peas and other things like that. We boys thought it was fun to eat food directly from our soil.

When we weren't playing war games you could usually find us riding bikes, or fishing, or hunting. Each spring a bunch of us repainted our bikes in our back yard. Since we used house-paint, we could tell how old our bikes were by the thick peeling layers of red, blue, green, orange and yellow.

Fishing on the river, our favorite lure was a piece of bread soaked and made into a ball to fit on the hook. We caught as many whitefish as we did trout. The elders of Bend held classes in the parks to teach us kids fishing methods and it started a life-long love of fly-fishing.

Other days we roamed around Awbrey Butte, armed with a single-shot .22 caliber rifle. Sometimes we actually shot a rodent, but for the most part our targets were pop cans propped up on a rock.

Not everything we did was safe. Although it was forbidden, we loved to sneak out for an afternoon and walk the "boom," a wooden sidewalk, extending upstream from the mills, floating in the center of the Deschutes River. Loggers used it to get up river and free log jams, but for the local kids, it was a source of excitement and exploration. If we chanced upon a logger he'd smile knowingly—maybe remembering what it was like to be a boy himself—and let us pass.

In looking back, it's obvious how much our lives were affected by the war during those years, but that didn't keep it from being a very special time for growing up in Bend.

Geordie Johnston b. 1934 in Coquille, Oregon. He moved to the Central Oregon area in 1939 and graduated from Redmond High School in 1949. After attending the University of Oregon, he served in the Air Force and became an airline pilot. He lives in Minnesota and returns to Central Oregon frequently to visit family, friends, and flyfish.

A "Sign" of Times to Come

Irene Carlson Bostelman

Never let it be said that Irene Bostelman didn't listen to her grandfather. "Own your own business," he always told her, "even if it is only a peanut stand." Irene and her first husband, Ted Carlson took that advice and bought an outdoor advertising company in Bend when they moved here from Spokane in 1948.

The business, which still prospers as Carlson Sign Company, was housed then in a run-down building behind the bus station on Irving Street. They had 6-8 employees at the time, and produced signs for businesses all over the tri-county area, as well as handling billboards for big national companies. Irene was active in the business and one of her jobs was to sit and count traffic on roads they were considering for billboard locations. "Sometimes," she said, "I could read a book between cars" —— a far cry from the complaints we all hear today about the traffic in Deschutes County!

There were traffic problems nevertheless. At that time, the route between Redmond and Bend was a narrow, two-lane road (the Old Bend-Redmond Highway), which claimed a number of lives each year. In an effort to make the road safer, Carlson Sign designed and placed a dramatic billboard along the road asking people to slow down and save lives.

In 1949, fifteen months after moving to Bend, Ted Carlson died, leaving Irene with a Colonial house on Congress Street, the business, the mortgage that went with it, and employees who counted on her. Irene told them that if they could handle the shop, she could handle the "business" side of things. In many respects she was a symbol, or a "sign", if you will, of times to come. At that point there weren't many women business owners or mangers, but under her guidance, Carlson Sign prospered and paid off its mortgage in the time originally planned. When asked what it was like to be a woman running a business in Bend in the early 50s, Irene said she felt she was well accepted. "And," she added, "it was fun."

In the mid-1950s, Irene's son, Dick, who had joined the Air Force after graduating from college, returned to Bend, and bought the business from her. Dick built a new building for Carlson Sign on Forbes Road in the early 1970s, where it is today. Almost 50 years later, Carlson Sign remains in the family and Irene's grandson, Peter, now runs the business.

In 1953 Irene married Hank Bostelman, one of the employees that came with the business in 1948. Hank and Irene enjoyed life. They traveled and played golf. The women's bridge club Irene started in 1950 still meets regularly and includes two ladies from the original group, herself and Doris Thomas. Irene and Hank were also one of about 50 couples who called themselves "The Little Club" and met twice a month for ballroom dancing. The big events were held in the ballroom of the old Pilot Butte Inn. Irene would probably still be dancing, but said that at her age it is tough to find partners.

At 93 years of age, Irene today is a small, stylish woman who lives comfortably in her home on the Deschutes River just north of downtown Bend. She still strides along, attends many events around Bend, and has many friends. While Bend has gotten larger, she really doesn't see significant changes from the beautiful, friendly place she came to 53 years ago.

One thing Irene misses is her car. Just having the car sitting in the garage gave me a sense of freedom. "Oh well, I'll just do without my wheels," she says. Irene was pleased to have seen the new millennium, and while she doesn't have any particular desire to live to 100, she says if she does, "she will try to be a good sport about it."

Irene (Carlson) Bostelman, b. 1907 in Minneapolis, Minnesota. She lived on Congress Street after moving to Bend in 1948. She owned Carlson Sign Company.

Growing Up In Bend Spoiled Us
Jim Crowell

My folks were born and raised in Minnesota. We came to Bend in 1940. A large percentage of the population of Bend had migrated from Minnesota, beginning in 1916 when the two large mills— Shevlin-Hixon and Brooks-Scanlon began operations. There were so many "Minnesotans" in the '40s that the Minnesota state picnic was the social event of the summer.

My family was typical for Bend in those years because my dad worked for the mills. My mom was a stay-at-home homemaker. We owned our own home, which was a three-room house we bought in 1943 for $500. My dad (on his own and with just simple hand tools) added two rooms in 1948. We didn't have a car until I was 16 because neither my dad or mom could drive and, most importantly, we couldn't afford one.

My dad worked in the woods for Brooks-Scanlon. He was a small man, a smoker, and not in good health. Being an edgerman was a tough job for him. An edgerman positioned the large, heavy boards coming off the head rig to have their barked edges cut off. Modern mills have sophisticated roller systems that make it relatively easy to maneuver the heavy boards. But in my dad's day, it was more a matter of leverage and strength. Dust in the mill wasn't controlled back then. That smoking and the dust, plus doing a job that was too much for a man of his size - well, it just broke him down, as it did a lot of other men of that era.

I started school as a first grader at St. Francis in downtown Bend. The basic education system was sound but there were the usual conflicts with the teachers - all of whom were Catholic nuns. I must admit, I probably had more problems with them than most of the other students because while I was raised as a Catholic and my mother was Catholic, my father wasn't. I inherited a strong streak of independence from him.

After one run-in with the school as a 7th grader, I began thinking of transferring to Kenwood. At that time, in the late 1940s, there was a very competitive grade school athletic program. It involved Kenwood and Allen public grade schools, St. Francis, and the eighth grade at Bend High School.

That winter, the Kenwood basketball coach - John Prentiss - found out I was considering moving to Kenwood. He had me come down to the Kenwood gym during the Christmas vacation and he "recruited" me to play at Kenwood.

When I went to St. Francis after the vacation and told Sister Superior that I was going to transfer to Kenwood, she called my mother and said they'd get things "straightened out" if I stayed at St. Francis. I agreed to stay but it wasn't long before I was in trouble again.

I took piano lessons at St. Francis. They had nice little practice rooms in the basement of the school. But, you were not allowed to play any music other than the prescribed lessons. The nuns would go from room to room making sure that we were all working on the appropriate pieces. Any kind of popular music was absolutely taboo.

Somehow, I got my hands on the sheet music to the hottest popular number of the day – "The Woody Woodpecker Song." After the nun left, I pulled out my Woody Woodpecker sheet music and started playing it. The next thing I knew she had doubled back to my room, came in, and rapped my knuckles with a ruler. It was obvious that it would be better for me to transfer, which I did...with no regrets, except I quit piano lessons and that has haunted me to this day.

My childhood and my teenage years were idyllic beyond the standard definition because of the kind of town Bend was at that time. The war was over, the national (and local) economy was booming, and the town was unrivaled for its pure beauty and charm.

Movies, stores, schools, and parks were within walking distance. People knew each other. And there were many things for kids to do that didn't require a lot of money. There were trout in the Deschutes at Drake Park and in Tumalo Creek. The banks were lined with kids all summer. The Bend Recreation Department was light years ahead of other towns, even in the 1940s, and had very full summer programs. For a lot of us, growing up in Bend spoiled us for the rest of our lives.

Jim Crowell, b. 1937 in Minnesota, moved to Bend in 1940. He attended Bend schools and has had a career in teaching and public relations. He is currently the Member Services Director for Central Electric Co-Op and an increasingly well known playwright.

First in the County - First in the State
Dorothy McClain

Being a commissioner, that was a tough one. I was a woman in a man's world. It wasn't easy for them to accept me, far from it. They tended to say, "Thanks honey, you go over there in that chair and look pretty." And you know that didn't happen.

I was born in the Sand Hills of Nebraska. I was born in 1917 and raised on a cattle ranch and dairy. We lived outside a small town of about fifteen hundred population. And of course it was Nebraska. You can imagine, in summer the windows filled up with sand, and in the winter they filled with snow. And those old thin windows.....and it was cold. We had a dairy farm and bottled and delivered our milk from 100 cows. I used to help Papa on the route and collections.

I was raised during the Depression. Nebraska in the Sand Hills with little to no water. In those days they didn't have the irrigation that we have now. We went through there not long ago, and it was green and beautiful. But it was dry when I was there. But, I never had any hardships, my father was considered rather well to do. My mother died when I was nine. My father raised my five brothers and me and was a stern man. To this day, I don't remember him kissing me, but I do remember him being very kind.

My father sent me to Iowa State after my high school graduation in 1935. That's were he sent me out of the clear blue. I studied bookkeeping and after graduation moved to Sheraton, Wyoming near a couple of my brothers. Later, I went to Tillamook. One brother, Clifton, graduated from Nebraska as a cheese maker, and was a cheese maker in Tillamook. During World War II, I worked at the rationing board. I was asked to take a job in the sheriff's office and that was where I met my first husband, Walt Smead. We moved to Bend where he was a state policeman.

On January 1, 1948, we purchased this 200-acre dairy farm out here on Butler Market Road and Powell Butte Highway. The State of Oregon Milk Control Board regulated price and production in those years. Those years when I was at the dairy were kind of a glory time in Bend. Several movies were made here. Our horses were always used. We would go out and wrangle and hire out on these movies. We became very well acquainted with Richard Boone. His son Peter would stay out at the dairy with us. The TV series "Have Gun... Will Travel" filmed around here for about 5 years.

After the dairy, I went to work for Les Schwab Tire. The word was out that a new county commissioner was going to be elected. Several people came to me and said that I should run and so I did. I didn't know very much about Bend back then. Sometimes the men would be in our planning meetings and they'd be talking about roads and what they were going to do. And I'd say, " Hey, just wait a minute. Where is that road?" And so I would get with a couple of the men and about 4 a.m., we'd go out to look at the roads so I'd be prepared to do battle with the men.

Along with other historians, I helped start the Deschutes County Historical Society. It all started when one of the commissioners said, "Well now honey, we're just going to tear those buildings down." They were talking about the ones on the corner of Greenwood and Harriman. I said, "Now just stop right now, we're not getting rid of that stone house, that's history!!" So we moved the county records from the halls in the County Courthouse to the stone building on the corner. That building later became the Historical Society's first museum.

I started the first Bend catering service in 1970 after people would say, "Oh, Dorothy, would you do this Christmas party for me?" Through the catering business, in 1972, I met Ken Cale and we were married.

Working like I did, with the role that I played, I certainly saw that Bend was growing. There was magic here. Sometimes I couldn't understand that magic. It does get cold and snowy. But Bend is beautiful and if you like to ski, cold and snowy is not a bad thing.

Dorothy McClain,b.1917 in Nebraska, moved to Bend from Tillamook in the late 1940s. In the early years she worked on the dairy and raised three children. She became the first woman county commissioner in Deschutes County and in the State of Oregon in 1965.

Lee Maker

Later Day Stage Driving:
The Reoccurring Drunk and Other Mishaps

Lee Maker

For 30 years Lee Maker drove the Mt. Hood Stage which later became the Trailways Bus Company.

Over the years I had two famous people on the bus. The first was Jimmy Stewart. He was down in Eugene where they were makin' a movie over there, and he wanted to look at the bus, so another guy and I showed him around. He even wanted to look at the engine and all that. Did you know he was a pilot too?

I used to haul Aunt Kate. Do you know her? She was the dance hall gal from Alaska, Klondike Kate. Not everyone knows it, but she lived in Bend for awhile and every time she'd ride the bus, she'd buy me a pack of cigarettes.

We weren't supposed to carry drunks on the bus, and that was always a problem. One day when one tried to get on I said, "No, I can't take ya." When I said that, he wanted to fight. Well, there was a taxi stand right next door to the bus depot so I told him that he could take a taxi to Redmond. He was all agitated and said, "I've got to get to Portland; my mother is dying." I had heard that story so many times that I wouldn't let him on. Then when we got to Redmond, there he was waiting for the bus. He came up to me and said, "I've got to get to Portland." And I said, "No I can't take you." And he said, "You're just like that guy in Bend. I would have licked him too, but my mother's dying and I gotta get to Portland!"

Another time when I kicked a guy off in Redmond, there was a woman sitting on the right front seat. She said, "Aren't you ashamed of yourself, kicking that poor man off. His mother is dying in Portland." So I said, "I'll go back and get him, if you will sit with him and make him behave himself." "No that's not my job," she replied. And I just had to say, "Well, I'm not going to give him to anybody else." After that I didn't hear another word out of her.

Another time...I don't know if I should tell you about this, but it was in Maupin, and we didn't have any air conditioning in those days. I pulled off the street onto a side street headed for a food stop. All the windows were all open and the people were sweating, so when we stopped everybody got off the bus. Then a cattle truck pulled up and parked right next to the bus. I mean it was as close as he could get, parked right beside of me.

Now, when you haul cattle they get the scours. You know what that is? It's in their digestive system and it's like taking a physic. Well, when they let loose, they hit every seat on that bus. All the windows were open and they pooped right in it you know. I came out after drinking some coffee and started to get in the bus when I saw all these people were standing on the sidewalk. And I said, "Why don't you get in?" "You go in there and look." they said. They might have added, "and smell it too," but they didn't have to. It was awful!

I got all the newspapers I could find in the restaurant there and cleaned them off the best I could, and then covered the seats up. The people got in and somehow we made it to Portland. My boss said, "Why didn't you clean that bus up?" I told him that it wasn't going to get clean unless we steam cleaned it, which we did. Oh, I'm tellin' ya, that was a mess.

Yeah, thirty-five years of driving and I saw some things - strange, interesting, funny, odd, you name it, but a lot of the same sort of things keep happening again and again. Fortunately, though, there was only one incident with a truck full of cattle that had the scours.

Harold Leland (Lee) Maker, b. 1921 in Prineville. After growing up and working in the logging camps he served in WWII. He was a Trailways bus driver for over 30 years and received a 3 Million-Mile Safe Driver Award. He currently lives in Bend.

I remember catching June bugs by the fruit jar full as did all the kids on the westside. Tied a thread around a leg and let them fly.

Iris (Stewart) Wood

Mt. Bachelor's First Snowcat
- Felix & Sons

Mount Bachelor - For the Love of Skiing

Felix Marcoulier

Before there were chair lifts Felix and Edla Marcoulier hiked up Mt. Bachelor and skied down. They would drive 12 hours nonstop to Sun Valley, Idaho and ski from dawn to dusk an entire week before returning home. "We were more than serious about skiing. We ski-jored behind cars growing up in Northern Minnesota," Felix said. No surprise then that this couple, raising a large family, operating a wholesale meat cutting business and dedicated to Bend from the moment they saw it, would get involved in the development of Mt. Bachelor.

The Marcouliers arrived in Bend on their honeymoon in June 1939. Except for vacations, they never left. Felix got a job as a meat cutter at Safeway on Wall Street in downtown Bend. "The meat cutting business those days was full service," said Felix. "You knew the customer, what they wanted and how they wanted it prepared. We delivered to the home."

Within six months, Felix went to work for the Bend Dairy Company on Greenwood Avenue where the skating rink now stands. The dairy was full-service with meat available for sale alongside dairy products. Felix ran the meat locker side of the operation. They had 400 cold storage lockers that could hold up to 200 pounds of meat each. Rent was $12 a year. Customers had their own keys and would walk into the meat locker to retrieve the cuts they wanted. Before large-capacity home refrigerator-freezers, it was easier for a meat company to keep the meat properly cooled than for individuals to do so at home. Most customers came by daily to pick up what they needed for dinner.

In 1943, Felix began separating the meat locker service from the Bend Dairy and developing the wholesale side of the business to better service large accounts, the biggest of which was the federal government. During WW II, there were 90,000 hungry troops in Central Oregon. "When Camp Abbot and the Redmond Airbase were at peak capacity, there were troops everywhere. You couldn't get a seat in a restaurant the town was so crowded. The war was very good for business, but price controls and ration-stamps made keeping records a fiasco," Felix said. "It was frustrating to consumers because everything had different point values. If they didn't have enough points they couldn't get the cut of meat they wanted." In 1945 Felix established the Mid-State Meat Company, which is still in business today

The upside to the war effort in Bend was the nightlife. The Pine Tavern and Pilot Butte Inn highlighted a growing number of restaurants and nightspots. "There were night clubs and dances everywhere," Marcoulier recalled. "We drove to all the Grange Halls including Gilchrist and Prineville to go dancing. Only The Dalles-California Highway was paved. It ran through downtown Bend. All other roads were dirt. Many people said Bend would fold after the war and they said it even more when the Shevlin-Hixon mill sold to Brooks-Scanlon in 1950, but I had faith. This was such a nice place to live."

Edla Marcoulier worked full time as a mother and housekeeper. She had eight children to raise and five houses to keep. "I worked 60-70 hours a week for the 32 years I was in the meat cutting business, but I always thought she worked harder than me," Felix said. All the Marcoulier kids attended St. Francis School and Bend High School.

In 1957, Felix let Bill Healy talk him into investing $10,000 in the newly formed Mt. Bachelor Ski Resort. "That was a pile of money back then," Felix recalled. Marcoulier was one of the five principal investors, along with Dr. Bradford Pease, Phil Gould, Oscar Murray and Healy. "We didn't know each other all that well before doing business." For 18 years Felix served on Mt. Bachelor's board of directors, four of them as treasurer. In its first year of operation, the resort offered two rope tows and a poma lift. It has steadily upgraded every year since.

A businessman at heart and keen observer of how other ski resorts were developed and operated, Marcoulier brought common sense to the budding ski resort, but making money wasn't his primary motive. "Personally, I just enjoyed skiing. It's a good family activity. At one point, all 10 of us were skiing. We weren't worried about promoting the business, although we knew it was having an effect. Cars started coming, everybody started getting excited. The Bulletin reported on it constantly."

From 1964-66, Marcoulier got so busy with Mt. Bachelor he "farmed out Mid-State Meat to someone else." Then in 1968 the meat company almost went bankrupt, forcing Felix back into his original line of work, but not before he oversaw construction and managed the only overnight accommodations on Mt. Bachelor.

There were two problems with overnight lodging at the mountain. People would go into town at night and then get their cars stuck on the way back blocking the snowplows. Also, the lodge couldn't fill the big demand for lodging. So it was converted it into a day lodge. It is the West Village Lodge. The original shape of the building Marcoulier designed and constructed is still apparent despite numerous remodels.

Marcoulier retired in 1975 from Mid-State Meat, passing the business to his son Don, who still runs it today. In 1976 he sold his interests in Mt. Bachelor to Dean Pape'. After that he just went skiing for fun.

Felix Marcoulier, b. 1917 in Minnesota came to Bend in 1939. He and his wife, Edla, raised 8 children and continue to live in Bend.

It's Been Quite A While
Grace Linton Elder

I've lived here quite a while, about 84 years. I was almost seven years old when we moved to Bend on Easter Sunday, 1916.

My father, Robert Stanley Linton, was a logging superintendent for Shevlin-Hixon Mill. He was gone all week, coming home each weekend. When a fire broke out I sometimes went with my father on weekends to walk the fire line and make sure the fire was out. I looked forward to these excursions with him. There was no fire fighting equipment in those days. We drove to the location in my father's Ford. The road was deeply rutted and very bumpy, so there was no sleeping in the car during the trip!

Our home was one of the first built on Congress St., about 1917. Most of the homes in this area were built for the mill bosses. Our house still stands at 514 Congress St. My father Robert put seven coats of varnish on all the woodwork throughout the house and I am told the woodwork has never been refinished. Some nice homes were also built for mill people on Delaware Street. I think that was the second residential street to be paved. Congress was the first and that happened about 1919 or 1920. There was a grassy area in the middle with a paved lane on each side.

Reid School, for grades one through six, was only two years old when I started there. I then attended junior high school on Lafayette Street. They were one-room buildings built on the side of the hill with a walkway leading up to them. The high school was a brick building in the same area, on what is now the wayside park near the courthouse. In my junior year we were moved into the new high school between Bond and Wall Streets, which is now the Bend-La Pine School District Administration Building.

During my junior high and early high school years we walked for physical education classes from school to the gym, which had been the Bend Athletic Club and is now the Boys' and Girls' Club. That involved walking to the gym, changing clothes, having class, changing back into our school clothes and walking back to school.

That was good exercise itself! Moving into the new high school cut this trip considerably. Students were not bussed to school in those days, and we walked home for lunch too.

The Bend Athletic Club was sold to the school district about 1919 for a dollar. The area upstairs facing Wall Street housed the city library. Prior to that space becoming available the library was in the home of Mrs. Lawrence, on Tumalo Street.

When I was a teen-ager, dances were held in the Hippodrome that was located where the new Bend Public Library Building is now. However, I couldn't attend those dances because my mother didn't approve. We did go to movies in either the Liberty on Bond St. or Capitol Theater on Wall Street. Most of the time we entertained groups of young people in our homes. My girl friends and I spent a lot of time in outdoor activities. We went climbing in the mountains and camped out. My senior year in high school a group of girls hiked up Pilot Butte every morning before school, summer and winter. There was no road then. If the weather was too bad, we walked on a route in town.

Following graduation from high school in 1927, I attended Reed College in Portland. I didn't want to go to Oregon State College or the University of Oregon where there were sororities and fraternities, because I didn't want to be a part of that social life. At the end of my junior year I left college to be married.

My husband's family came to the area in 1919, settling on a ranch on the Old Bend Redmond Highway. Joe came from a family of nine children, while I had only one sister, who was seven years younger than me. I didn't meet my future husband until I was home from college because he attended school in Redmond

I remember Joe had an Oldsmobile Sport Roadster, which was really impressive! He worked on the railroad at Brooks-Scanlon Mill. However, it wasn't long until my father got him away from the competition and into a job at Shevlin-Hixon, where he remained until it closed.

I have always been involved in activities with young people. I worked with the Campfire Program from 1923 until 1963. We started with eleven girls and grew to over six hundred. Around 1949-1950 I began the PTA at Kenwood School.

We began the school lunch program at Kenwood and bought the curtain for the stage in the gym. We were really proud of that velvet curtain which may still be there. Both parents attended the meetings, but the dads came for the good refreshments, except perhaps Joe Slate who I later persuaded to start the PTA at Allen School

As I said, I've lived here quite awhile. I am 91 now and most of my old friends are gone, but I still live alone in my own home, am active and enjoy life. Sometimes I feel down, but when I do I start a new book and lose myself in the story. I've always been an avid reader and I long ago discovered that good stories, like good memories, bring great pleasure.

Grace (Linton) Elder, b. 1909 in St. Paul, Minnesota and moved to Central Oregon at age 7. She attended Reid School and Bend High School before working as a bookkeeper for Miller Lumber Company.

The future is something which everyone reaches at the rate of sixty minutes an hour, whatever he does, whoever he is.

C.S. Lewis

The great thing about getting older is that you don't lose all the other ages you've been.

Madeline L'Engle

The man who views the world at 50 the same as he did at 20 wasted 30 years of Life.

Muhammad Ali

We Never Meant to Stay
Becky Johnson

It's been a path of time and circumstance that brought Sam and me to Central Oregon - "temporarily" - in 1947; and it has led to calling it "home" for over fifty years. And we never intended to stay in the first place.

To begin, Sam was born and grew up in Berkeley, California. I was born in Fort Wayne, Indiana, and grew up in Bellevue, Ohio. It was WW II that brought us together.

Sam was with the Army Corp of Engineers and ran a lumber products purchasing and shipping department for the Pacific Theater. I was one of three WAVE officers doing recruiting in Oregon, and part of Washington and Idaho.

Most important to Sam and me was our meeting and being married in Portland in 1944. We vowed that, once the war was over, we would come back to Oregon and live in Portland. That was a whole year away. Meanwhile, I had orders to go Texas, then Astoria, and then Seattle before we were "separated" from the service in 1946. That's when we moved to a Portland apartment.

Sam and his father were "partners" with two other men in a sawmill and logging business in Sisters. Sam found himself slipping and sliding over the mountains to Redmond, Tygh Valley and Sisters while I was working for volunteer agencies in Portland. So one Thursday in 1947, we looked at each other and said, "This is crazy. Why don't we move to Redmond - temporarily, of course?"

We moved into a one-bedroom apartment at the El Rancho Motel, then Redmond's "finest." It was "furnished" and we could "entertain", modestly. After about a year of that, we found a small house. Not much larger than the El Rancho "digs" but it had a yard and garden and a chance to "decorate". We did the latter through correspondence and pictures to an interior decorator friend of mine who worked for the large Higbee Department Store in Cleveland.

He had drapes and curtains made, carpets cut and ready for laying, upholstery and bed-covers selected and made and sent out to Redmond.

Sam was a partner in the Tite Knot Sawmill. In the late 1940s the partners bought timberland near Burns. Since Sam and I were the only ones of the three partners who did not have children, we were to move to Burns to build and run a sawmill. We even selected a house. And then, two things happened that changed our lives and kept us in the heart of Central Oregon: one, the partners sold the Burns timber to the Hines Lumber Company; and two, we were going to have a baby.

We needed a larger house. We decided to build on the north rim of the canyon and bought two unimproved lots. We found an architect and set him to work. That was June of 1950 and the baby was due on the scene the end of December. Pretty tight schedule - especially for novices with two immensely important "firsts" - building the first house and having the first child.

Then another fateful turning of the road: the older JR Roberts and his wife (JR was one of Redmond's "founding fathers") decided that the big old Roberts homestead was too large and demanding, and they would like to live in a smaller place. Their son Maurice and his wife Lovelle, were part-way finished with building a house on the east rim of the canyon and they wanted to sell it and move into the Roberts homestead.

What better for us than to sell our small house to JR and buy the younger Maurice Roberts' unfinished home. So on a hot day in August, 1950, we all moved, in a three-way shift. 415 SW Canyon Drive became "home" to Sam and me - and to Betsy, born January 1951, and Patti, born 1953. It was originally intended to be an "interim" home base. We were always going to move back to Portland.

Then, another "fork in the road". In 1964, our State Representative Kessler Cannon resigned in order to buy radio station KBND.

Sam, who had never intended to get into politics was "drafted" to run for the Oregon House. Sam had never been much involved in Oregon politics; that had been one of my interests. No one really thought Sam could win against a very popular Madras incumbent. However, he did, and served seven terms in the Oregon Legislature. Governor Hatfield appointed me to the State Board of Higher Education and we both were knee-deep in local and state government.

When Sam retired from the Legislature in 1979, he was again asked to run for Redmond Mayor and served in that capacity until his sudden death in 1984.

All the Johnsons love the Northwest and especially Central Oregon. All of us are, indeed, fortunate and grateful that we live in a most unique and very special part of Oregon and can call it "home". For an "outsider" and a newcomer - fifty odd years ago - I'm glad we changed "temporarily" to "permanently".

Elizabeth (Becky) H. Johnson, b. 1913 in Indiana came to Central Oregon in 1947. She was a teacher and an officer in the Navy WAVES. She and her husband Sam have always been outstanding civic leaders in numerous state and regional activities. Mrs. Johnson continues in many philanthropic efforts including the Samuel S. Johnson Foundation.

In front of Cabin on the Deschutes:
Becky and Mother, Lydia

Order Form
The River Flows as the Mountains Watch
Deschutes Memories

Name _____ Phone (____)_____

Organization/Business_____

Address _____

City/State/Zip_____

Date _____

Payment: Check (Make Checks Payable to RSVP)
      Credit Card
      Visa/Mastercard Number_____ Exp._____
      Card Holder Signature_____

Quantity	Price	Total
	$15.00/book	

Plus Shipping/ Handling **$2.50 per book**
Please allow 5-7 working days for delivery

Order Total

Send Payment & Order Form to:

    RSVP/St. Charles Medical Center
    2500 NE Neff Road, Bend, OR 97701

Order by phone: (541) 388-7746
Fax orders to: (541) 385-6346
Order on-line: www.stcharlesfoundation.org

Proceeds go to support RSVP programs.